Forsyth County

৵ North Carolina ৲

FIRST COURT HOUSE.

Adelaide L. Fries

HERITAGE BOOKS
2008

HERITAGE BOOKS

AN IMPRINT OF HERITAGE BOOKS, INC.

Books, CDs, and more—Worldwide

For our listing of thousands of titles see our website
at
www.HeritageBooks.com

A Facsimile Reprint
Published 2008 by
HERITAGE BOOKS, INC.
Publishing Division
100 Railroad Ave. #104
Westminster, Maryland 21157

Originally published
Winston:
Stewarts' Printing House
1898

International Standard Book Numbers
Paperbound: 978-0-7884-1236-3
Clothbound: 978-0-7884-7517-7

CONTENTS.

PAGE.

THE EVOLUTION OF FORSYTH COUNTY...... 3

FIRST SETTLEMENT OF WACHOVIA............ 17

WACHOVIA AND THE REVOLUTIONARY
WAR.. 33

THE TITLE TO WACHOVIA.......................... 40

KERNERSVILLE. FRIEDBERG. FRIED-
LAND. HOPE 47

THE COURT HOUSE TRACT.......................... 53

NAMING THE COUNTY TOWN 67

FORSYTH COUNTY COURTS............................ 72

COUNTY MILITIA... 82

FORSYTH AND THE CIVIL WAR...................... 89

TOWNSHIP LINES.. 107

FORSYTH COURT HOUSE.............................. 119

ILLUSTRATIONS.

FORSYTH COUNTY............................Frontispiece

GRANTS TO SIR ROBERT HEATH AND
THE EIGHT LORDS PROPRIETORS, facing
page.. 4

THE EVOLUTION OF FORSYTH COUNTY,
facing page... 14

PROPOSED PLAN OF SALEM, facing page.. 26

FIRST COURT HOUSE, facing page................ 76

WINSTON AND SALEM CORPORATION
LINES, facing page...................................... 114

FORSYTH COURT HOUSE, facing page.......... 118

FORSYTH COUNTY.

NOT all that has disappeared from view is lost forever; not all that is forgotten can be no more remembered. Lord Bacon says that "by an exact and scrupulous diligence and observation, out of monuments, names, words, proverbs, traditions, p r i v a t e records and evidences, fragments of stories, passages of books that concern not story, and the like," it is possible to "save and recover somewhat from the deluge of time."

Forsyth stands not upon the page of history blood-red with battle or pale with the counsels of the nations, yet behind her and around her lies the story of a commonwealth, and within her borders men have lived and wrought, have served their God, their State, their

Country faithfully, even as where the trumpet notes of fame have called all men to witness.

Now she stands forth, crowned with the majesty of years of growth and ever widening influence, and bids the pen unfold the Past, and give to these her children the record of her life, nor let her quiet days of joy and sorrow, struggle and achievement, sink all unheeded into the dust of ages.

CHAPTER I.

THE EVOLUTION OF FORSYTH COUNTY.

On October 30th, 1629, King Charles I, of England, gave to Sir Robert Heath, his Attorney General, that portion of the American Continent, stretching from the Atlantic to the Pacific, between the degrees of latitude 36 and 31, or from a line that would pass through Durham, N. C., almost to the southern boundary of Georgia. This land was called *Carolina* in honor of King Charles, the portion of the continent to the south bearing the name of *Florida*, " Land of Flowers."

No active steps were taken towards establishing a colony there, and so, on March 24th, 1663, Charles II gave Carolina to eight English Lords, deciding that Robert Heath's title was forfeited by his neglect of the province. A little later it was discovered that about thirty-one miles were left between the 36° and the Virginia line, and therefore on June 30th, 1665, a second Patent was given the Lords Proprietors extending their boundaries to 36° 30″ on the north, where it met Virginia, and to 29° on the south.

The first settlements were naturally along the sea coast, travel by land being slow and difficult, and the first *County* to be established was *Clarendon*, in the neighborhood of Cape Fear ; *Albemarle County* on Albemarle Sound following very shortly. It was the intention to form another county—Craven—south of Cape Romain, (including the harbors of Charleston and Port Royal,) but this was not carried out.

Clarendon promised well at first, but a settlement from New England and two from the Barbadoes failed in succession, and the county was practically abandoned for a number of years, Albemarle'

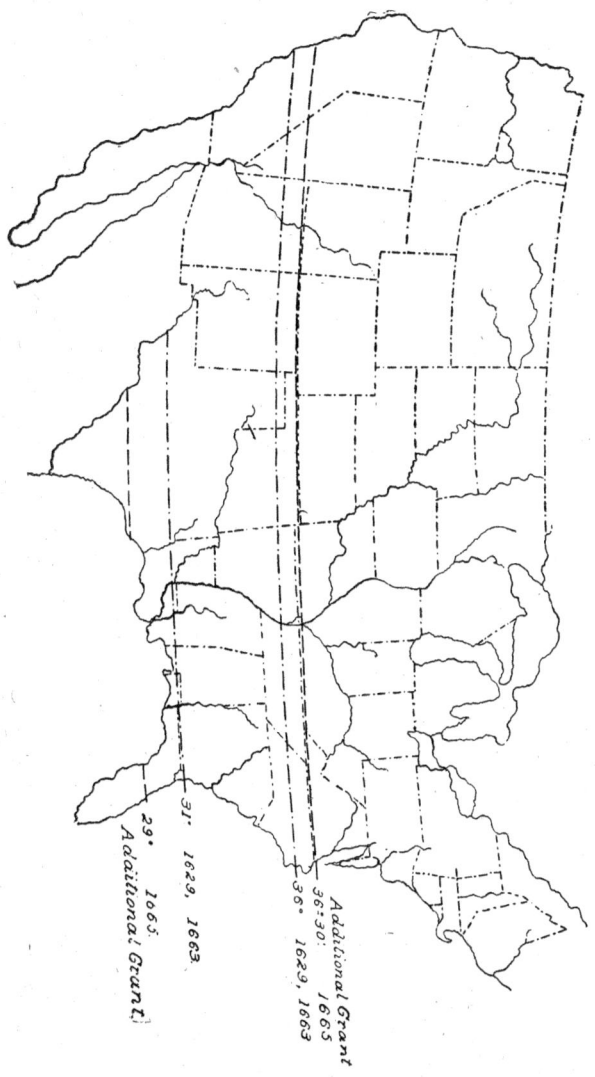

Grants to Sir Robert Heath 1629, — and the eight
Lords Proprietors 1663 and later in 1665.

31° 1629, 1663

29° 1665
Additional Grant.

36°30' 36°30'
36° 1629, 1663

Additional Grant
1665

4a

being the seat of government and the only one appearing in the records.

By the end of 1696, a settlement had sprung up on " Pampticoe River " (Pamlico Sound), and on December 9th, the *County of Bath* was erected. It gradually grew southward to the Neuse and Cape Fear Rivers, taking the place of the extinct County of Clarendon. Like Albemarle, the County of Bath was divided into " Precincts," practically settlements scattered in different parts of the county and each entitled to certain representation in the General Assembly. Of these Precincts, *New Hanover*, formed in 1729, was near the mouth of the Cape Fear River. Until comparatively modern times the boundaries of Precincts and Counties were not carefully surveyed lines, but the growth from a settlement would in a manner retain a connection with it, until, having attained a considerable size, it would desire its own representation and rights ; thus the growth up the Cape Fear River from New Han-

over in 1734 became *Bladen Precinct*,
named for Martin Bladen, a member of
the Board of Trade.

In 1738, the names of Albemarle and
Bath were dropped, and the Precincts
became Counties.

Then the settlement spread from Bladen County on the Cape Fear, to the
Pee Dee or lower Yadkin, and became a
separate county in 1749, under the name
of *Anson*, who at one time lived in Carolina, and was raised to the Peerage for
his brilliant services in the Spanish war.

With Anson County came the beginning of definite boundaries, and Anson
extended from the South Carolina line
to Virginia, the line dividing it from
Bladen being about " equi-distant from
Saxpahaw River (Haw River) and Great
Pee Dee River," and it was enacted that
" all the inhabitants to the westward of
the afore-mentioned dividing line, shall
belong and appertain to Anson County."

But by this time the Government of
Carolina had changed hands. Originally

" North Carolina " was only the thirty-
mile strip next to Virginia given to the
Proprietors by their second Charter, all
the rest being "Carolina"; then in course
of time settlements in the far south of
their possessions became " South Carolina," and the term "North Carolina"was
widened until it covered the territory
from Virginia to South Carolina, and
from the Atlantic to the Pacific, nomi-
nally, although in fact it never crossed
the Mississippi.

In 1710 Governors were appointed
separately for North and South Carolina,
and in 1719 South Carolina, tired of Pro-
prietory government, threw it off, claim-
ing and receiving the protection of the
Crown. North Carolina, on the other
hand, moved on in a sturdy, independ-
ent fashion, her Assembly making such
laws as it thought best, and obeying the
Proprietors' Governor until he became
unendurable, and then deposing him,
and welcoming the next incumbent.

But the original Proprietors died, and

their heirs found Carolina a poor invest-
ment and a troublesome charge; in 1728,
therefore, the holders of seven of the
eight equal undivided shares proposed to
sell all their interest in Carolina to the
Crown, and the proposition was accepted.
John, Lord Carteret, afterwards Earl
Granville, decided to retain his one-
eighth of the property, but gave up all
claim to the sovereignty. Although
South Carolina had thrown off the rule
of the Proprietors their landed rights
were unquestioned, and all the territory
granted by the Charters of Charles II
was involved in the purchase, the Crown
paying £2,500 for each of the seven
shares, and an additional £5,000 for
unpaid quit rents—a total of £22,500,
or about $112,500.

Lord Granville asked that his share
be laid off for him wherever a committee,
appointed half by himself and half by
the Crown, should decide. This petition
" his majesty was pleased to refer to the
right honorable the lords of the commit-

tee of his majesty's most honourable
privy council ", they referred it to " the
lords commissioners for trade and plantations ", they reported to the privy council, and they reported to his majesty,
some twelve years after the petition was
offered. But the report being favorable,
and his majesty approving, a committee
was appointed to select the location, and
in 1744 Lord Granville received his
share from George II, then reigning. It
was " in the province of North Carolina,
next adjoining and contiguous to the
province of Virginia," and was " bounded
to the north by the line that divides Carolina from Virginia, to the east by the
great western ocean, commonly so called
(Atlantic), and as far southwardly as a
cedar stake set upon the sea-side in the
latitude of 35° 34'' north latitude, *   *
from that stake by a west line *   * as
far as the bounds of the charter granted
to the lords proprietors of Carolina."
This land was granted to " John, Lord
Carteret, his heirs and assigns forever,"

they "yielding and paying to his said
majesty, his heirs and successors the
annual rent of 1£ 13s 4d, payable at the
feast of All Saints, forever: and also
one-fourth part of all gold and silver ore
that shall be found."

On March 27th, 1753, that part of
Lord Granville's property lying in Anson
County was formed into a separate
county under the name of *Rowan*, so
called from Matthew Rowan, at that time
President of the General Assembly and
Chief Executive of the Province, Gov-
ernor Johnston having died, and Gov-
ernor Dobbs having not yet come. The
Act provided—

"That Anson County be divided by a line,
to begin where Anson line was to cross Earl
Granville's line, and from thence, in a direct
line north, to the Virginia line; and that the
said County be bounded to the north by the
Virginia line, and to the south by the south-
ern-most line of Earl Granville's land : * * *
and that all the inhabitants to the westward
of the said line, and included within the
before mentioned boundaries shall belong and
appertain to Rowan County."

These were the first straight, definitely surveyed lines in the history of the Counties; and the Granville line may be seen on a modern map of North Carolina, in the line which divides Moore, Montgomery, Stanly and Cabarrus, from Randolph, Davidson, Rowan and Iredell.

On December 5th, 1770, the Assembly held at New-Bern, Wm. Tryon being Governor, passed an Act by which, on April 1st, 1771, the northern part of Rowan County became *Surry County*, named for Lord Surry, a leading member of the Whig party in England. Guilford County, which then included Rockingham and Randolf, had been erected earlier in the same session of the Assembly; the boundaries of Surry County therefore began

"at a point forty-two miles north of Earl Granville's line, on Guilford County line; thence running north to the Virginia line; thence westwardly along the mountains to the ridge that divides the waters of the Yadkin and the Catawba rivers; thence along the said ridge to the northwest corner of Rowan county ; thence east along Rowan county line to the beginning."

The southern line was altered in 1773, and the western boundary was changed in 1777, when Wilkes County was formed from part of Surry and part of the District of Washington, the rest of that District becoming the County of Washington, now the State of Tennessee.

In the records of the General Assembly held at Fayetteville, on November 2nd, 1789, Samuel Johnston being Governor, this Act appears :

"WHEREAS, The large extent and inconvenient situation of the County of Surry, render the attendance of the inhabitants of the extreme parts at courts, elections and general musters, difficult and expensive : For remedy whereof, and to gratify the wishes of the good people of the county : 1. *Be it enacted, etc.,* That from and after the passing of this act, the county of Surry shall be divided into two distinct counties, by a line beginning on the line dividing this State from the State of Virginia, at a point equi-distant from the nearest parts of the counties of Rockingham and Wilkes, and running from thence until it intersects the Rowan county line, so as to leave an equal number of acres in each county. 2. *And be it further enacted*, That all that part of the said county, lying west of said line, shall be erected into a distinct county by the name of Surry county; and all that part lying east of said line, shall be erected into another distinct county by the name of *Stokes County*."

This name was given in honor of Colonel, afterwards Judge John Stokes, brother of Governor Montford Stokes.

The line between Surry and Stokes Counties seems originally to have run south by survey until it touched the Yadkin River the second time, and then, according to custom, to have followed the river to Rowan County. In this distance the river curved to the west and back again, forming a large C. In 1797 "all that part of the county of Stokes lying south of the Yadkin river" was added to Surry, and when, later, the southern part of Surry was erected into Yadkin County, this segment, cut off by the river from the county to which it belonged, became popularly known as "Little Yadkin." The Act of 1797 gave

a straight and definite line from the bend
of the Yadkin south, but to go north
directly from the bend, according to the
Act of 1789, gave to Stokes a narrow,
ragged strip of land on the west of the
river; in 1811, therefore, the line was
changed, and it was enacted—

"That after the county line intersects the
southern boundary of the lands formerly
belonging to Samuel Kirby, senior, now Joseph Wilson, it shall run thence along the
southern and western boundaries of said land
to the Yadkin river; thence up the river until
it intersects the present line between the two
counties."

During the session of Assembly in the
winter of 1848–1849, Stokes County was
divided by an Act that read as follows:

"Whereas, the extent and peculiar situation
of the county of Stokes render it desirable,
with a large majority of its inhabitants, to
have the same divided : Sec. 1. *Be it enacted
by the General Assembly of the State of North
Carolina, and it is hereby enacted by the
authority of the same*, That, from and after
the passing of this act, the county of Stokes
shall be divided into two distinct counties, by
a line beginning at the south-west corner of

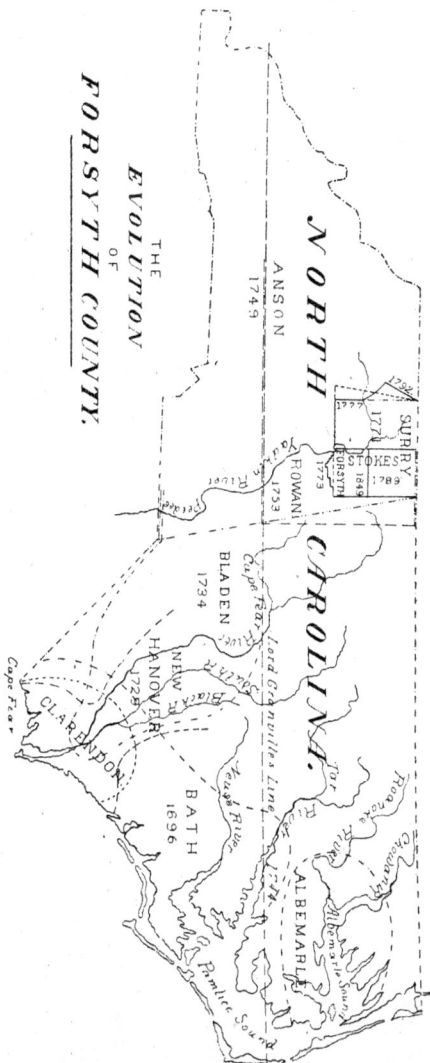

THE
EVOLUTION
OF
FORSYTH COUNTY.

NORTH CAROLINA.

ANSON
1749

SURRY
1771

STOKES
1789

SURRY
1773

ROWAN
1753

FORSYTH
1849

BLADEN
1734

NEW
HANOVER
1729

CLARENDON

BATH
1696

ALBEMARLE

Lord Granville Line

Cape Fear River

Yadkin River

Blue Ridge

Cape Fear

Neuse River

Pamlice Sound

Albemarle Sound

Roanoke River

Chowan River

14a

Rockingham county, and running thence west to the Surry county line.

Sec. 2. *And be it further enacted*, That all that part of the said county, lying north of said line, shall be erected into a distinct county by the name of Stokes county ; and all that part lying south of said line, shall be erected into another distinct county by the name of *Forsyth county*, in honor of the memory of Col. Benjamin Forsyth, a native of Stokes county, who fell on the Northern frontier in the late war with England."

Col. Forsyth was born in Stokes County, and was a member of the North Carolina Legislature in 1807-8. He was appointed a lieutenant of infantry from North Carolina, and became a captain of riflemen in 1808. During the war of 1812, he commanded in the successful assault on Gananoque, Upper Canada, and won his rank as lieutenant-colonel at the capture of the British Guard at Elizabethtown. He also distinguished himself at the capture of Fort George, and at the attack on York. He was killed in battle with a superior force of British and Indians, near Oldtown, N. Y., on June 28th, 1814.

An Act, supplemental to the one dividing Stokes County, gave a number of particulars as to the formation of the county government, etc., and appointed Caleb Jones, Frederick C. Meinung and John Banner to run the dividing line. The third section of the Act provided—

"That Zadok Stafford, John Stafford, Henry A. Lemly, Leonard Conrad and Francis Fries, be appointed commissioners for the county of Forsyth, whose duty it shall be to select suitable sites for permanent seats of justice in their respective counties [Stokes commissioners were also appointed]; to purchase * * * tracts of land on which to erect the necessary public buildings; to lay off the residue, not used for public purposes, in streets and town lots; to sell such lots at public auction; * * to purchase for and at each court-house not less than thirty acres of land. Sec. 4. That the title to the said tracts of land obtained by said commissioners shall be made to the chairman of the county court of county in which such land is situated, and his successors."

The Act dividing Stokes was ratified on January 16th, 1849, which might be called the birthday of Forsyth County.

CHAPTER II.

FIRST SETTLEMENT IN WACHOVIA.

Some ninety-seven years before the erection of Forsyth County, a traveler from beyond the seas came to Carolina. Nathaniel Rice was at that time the Chief Executive of the Province, having been President of the Council on July 17th, 1752, when Governor Johnston died, and being in his turn succeeded, January 29th, 1753, by Matthew Rowan, already referred to in connection with the naming of Rowan County.

The visitor, Bishop Joseph Spangenberg, came as the representative of the UNITAS FRATRUM, or Moravian Church, which had its headquarters at Herrnhut, Saxony, and was considering the purchase of a tract of land from Lord Granville, in order to establish a settlement in Carolina. His mission was to find,

2

somewhere in Lord Granville's land, a
well watered and fertile spot, where some
100,000 acres could be secured in a com-
pact body, and towns could be built and
governed according to Moravian ideas.
After searching all the northern part of
the State, from the ocean to the mountains, and into Tennessee, he found such
a place as he desired; it was surveyed
under his direction, and, on August 7th,
1753, Lord Granville conveyed the "Wachovia Tract" by 19 deeds to James
Hutton, of London, who had been
selected to hold the title to the land.

According to the agreement of the
same date between "the Right Honorable John Earl Granville Viscount Carteret and Baron Carteret of Hawnes,"
and "James Hutton, Gentleman, Secretary to the Unitas Fratrum,"—with the
approval of the Lord Advocate (then
Count Zinzendorf), the Chancellor and
the Agent of the Unitas Fratrum—Granville, "in consideration of the sum of
Five Hundred pounds Sterling   *   *

conveyed to the said James Hutton, his heirs and assigns (in Trust and for the Use, Benefit and Behoof of the said Unitas Fratrum) * * the full quantity of Ninety-Eight Thousand Nine Hundred and Eighty-Five Acres of land lying in the county of Anson * * under the yearly Rent or Sum of 148£, 9s. 2½d, (3 shillings per hundred Acres)." If any gold or silver mines were found ¼ was reserved for the King, and ½ of the remaining ¾ for Lord Granville. The rent was to be paid semi-annually, or annually if they preferred, and if it became six months overdue, the title was to be forfeited. Four years were allowed for the payment of the 500£, the 4 per cent. interest being paid with the rent. The 98,985 acres in 19 tracts were surveyed by Wm. Churton, and the deeds "Sealed and delivered in the presence of Arthur Dobbs and Ben Wheatley."

The Unitas Fratrum had no available funds to support so large an enterprise, but individual members and outside friends subscribed an amount sufficient " for locating and surveying the Land, for the payment of the Purchase Money and the yearly Quit rent of 148£, 9s., 2½d Sterl,   *   *   and still larger sums for the transportation of Settlers from Europe, most of them Germans, over Sea to Pennsylvania and thence by Land to North Carolina, as well as to settle and stock Trades." These good friends were gradually reimbursed by the proceeds of the sale of lands not needed for the Moravian towns.

The Wachovia Tract having been transferred into the hands of the Unitas Fratrum, the next step was to settle their new possessions, and for this purpose a party of twelve single Brethren left Bethlehem, Pa., on October 8th, 1753. These pioneers were:

Rev. Bernhard Adam Grube—the first Pastor,

Jacob Losch (Lash)—Business Manager,

Hans Martin Kalberlahn—Physician,

John Beroth and John Lisher—Farmers,

Herman Losh—Miller,

Jacob Lung—Gardener,

Christopher Merkle—Baker,

Erich Ingebresten—Carpenter,

Henry Feldhausen — Carpenter and Hunter,

Hans Peterson—Tailor,

Jacob Pfeil—Shoemaker.

" In a wagon with six horses they carried the various articles needed for their journey," and to provide the necessary food " some of their number would go to farms, sometimes ten miles off their road, and help to thresh the oats" besides paying for what they took away. " Not unfrequently they had to unload and carry a portion of their baggage over the mountains. They generally prepared their frugal morning meal at three o'clock, and started by the dawn of day, after their regular morning prayer." On November 13th, they crossed the Carolina line, and " on Saturday, the 17th of

November, 1753, at three o'clock P. M.,
they reached the spot where stands to
this day the town of *Bethabara*, now
commonly called *Old Town.*" "Here
they found shelter in a small cabin, built
and previously inhabited by a German of
the name of Hans Wagner, but then
unoccupied." On Sunday they rested,
but on the following day went energeti-
cally to work, and the little clearing soon
became a center of attraction to all the
surrounding country, the services of the
physician and tailor especially being
greatly needed by the scattered and
badly equipped population.

In Carolina, copying the mother-coun-
try, the Church of England was for many
years the established church. Each
county was constituted a Parish, with a
Vestry which had charge of the spiritual
affairs of the Parish, kept the register of
births and marriages, etc. While individual liberty of worship was usually not
interfered with, this supervision was
unpleasant to the Moravians, who had a

very complete system of their own for the government of their congregations and towns. Wachovia was still under the care of the church authorities in Bethlehem, Pa., and they took advantage of the coming of Arthur Dobbs, the new Governor for North Carolina, to petition special favor in the matter.

To Governor Arthur Dobbs.

MAY IT PLEASE YOUR EXCELLENCY:

Whereas, His Majesty and the late British Parliament in the year 1749 have thought proper to pass an Act in favor of the people known by the name of Unitas Fratrum, in order to encourage them to settle in the British Plantations in America. * * * And whereas, since that time the Lord Advocate, Chancellor, and Agent of the Unitas Fratrum have purchased a large Tract of Land, now called by them Wachovia, * * in order to settle a number of United Brethren thereon. And whereas, we and our United Brn. value nothing so much as Liberty of Conscience, and the granting an unlimited Liberty of Conscience to our people will prove a proper encouragement to transplant themselves from these and other parts to North Carolina.

Therefore, we the Subscribers, in behalf of our United Brn. who are already settled on

the said land called Wachovia, or have a mind
from time to time to settle there, pray, that
your Excellency may be pleased to recommend
to his Majesty's Council, and the General
Assembly of N. C. to pass an Act for the further encouragement of the people known by
the name of Unitas Fratrum to settle in the
province of N. C. whereby the land called
Wachovia may be erected into a separate Parish, and that leave be given to regulate the
matters in said Parish according to the Rules,
Rites, and Forms of our ancient episcopal
protestant church, which when so granted,
will not only be an undoubted encouragement
for our Brn. to settle themselves readily in the
province of N. C. but also cause us to promote
our Brn's removing from these Northern parts
to the said land Wachovia, and at the same
time impress a deep sense of gratitude upon
the minds of

Your Excellencys
most obliged &

Bethlehem in   most obedient
the county of   humble servants
Northampton &
Province of Penn.   DAVID EP.
19th Aug. 1754.   MATTHEW EPISC.

With this petition from Bishop David
Nitschmann and Bishop Matthew Hehl
went a letter from Peter Boehler, then
in Edenton, who most heartily recom-

mended the measure to Gov. Dobbs, urging that it asked only what all the northern Moravian settlements enjoyed, and
stating that without this privilege it
would be almost impossible to induce
more of the Brethren to move there.

The petition met with a kindly recep-
tion, and the General Assembly, in session in October, 1755, passed an Act
erecting Wachovia into a separate and
distinct Parish, which received the name
of *Dobbs Parish.* The success of this
measure meant much to the new settlement, and ultimately had great weight
in establishing the boundaries of the
county.

Meantime the Brethren went quietly
on with their work, a grist-mill and
meeting-house were erected, and at the
close of 1756, there were in the little
town 18 married people, 44 single Brethren, 1 boy, and 2 infants—65 in all.

The Indian War disturbed the following years, but brought Bethabara prom-
inently before the people, many coming

long distances to buy the grain which
the Brethren continued to sell at the
usual price, and many others availing
themselves of the protection afforded by
the fortifications, which had been thrown
up around the village, and around the
mill. Some of these visitors desiring to
connect themselves with the Moravians,
it was decided to begin another town,
and a suitable location having been found
three miles northwest of Bethabara,
about 2,000 acres were set apart for the
use of the *Bethania* congregation, and in
July, 1759, eight married couples from
Bethabara, and as many friends, settled
in their new home.

From the first it was the intention to
establish a town in the very center of
the Tract, and the name which they gave
to their first village, "Bethabara—House
of Passage," indicates that they considered it only as the stepping stone to this
central town. Peace having been
restored by 1762, and a number of additional settlers having come to Wachovia,

Scala von 160 Ruthen ie 16½ foot Englisch.

Muthmaßgebliches Project zu einer Stadt in North Carolina.

A. Capelle, Gemeinsaal.
B. Sechs Chorhäuser.
C. Apostolische Gemeinlogis und Gemeingericht.
E. Die Strassen und Baumalleen.
D. Strasse und Allee rund um den ersten Theil der Stadt.
F. Strasse und Allee rund um die Stadt.
G. ...
H. Vier Quartes zum Gottesacker.
K. Nicht Gassen mit Alleen.

it became possible to carry out this plan, and on February 14th, 1765, the site was selected by "lot." Five situations were chosen, all apparently suitable for the purpose, and then, according to their custom, the final choice was left with the Lord, the result being that *Salem* (as Count Zinzendorf had wished it to be named) was placed where it stands to-day.

In the Archives at Herrnhut, Germany, there is a plot—a "Project zu einer Stadt in North Carolina." In the center stands the Church, about it in a circle six Choir Houses, the Apothecary Shop, and the Inn and church offices. Between these buildings run eight streets diverging at equal angles, and each has rows of shade trees, and ten town lots, five on a side; then comes a circular avenue, and ten more lots on each street. Narrow streets pass at the rear of the lots, and divide the intervening sections, of which the one lying toward the east is occupied by the "Gottesacker"—

"God's Acre." A second circular avenue encloses the whole. Such was the
manner in which it was proposed to build
Wachovia's principal town, when as yet
it had not even a name, but when the
time came the land seemed unsuited for
it, and Forsyth County failed to receive
what would have been a unique and
attractive sight for later generations.

On January 6th, 1766, the first log
was cut for the first house to be built in
Salem, and on February 19th, eight
young men moved there, killing two
deer on their way through the woods.
Next day their surveyor, Reuter, laid
out the Square of the future town.

In 1768 Frederick William von Marshall came with his family to settle in
Salem, and from that time until the close
of the century he was the central figure
in the history of Wachovia. When the
Unitas Fratrum bought land in the New
World, the Quit Claim deeds were made
in the name of some individual member
(as James Hutton, of London, for Wa-

chovia), and the management rested with the German Board. As the American Province increased in size it became necessary to have a representative of the Board there; a Power of Attorney was therefore sent by Hutton to Marshall, who was then on an official visit to Bethlehem, Pa., authorizing him to take charge of the affairs of the Unity in Wachovia, and especially to *lease* lands in the manner he should find most advantageous.

In pursuance of these instructions Marshall visited Wachovia in the fall of 1764, being present in February, 1765, when the site for Salem was chosen; then returned to Europe, where arrangements were made for him to become a resident of Salem. An order from " the Lord Advocate of Unitas Fratrum, Henry XXVIII (Henry XXVIII Reuss, Count and Lord of Plauen), Abraham v. Gersdorff, Chancellor of the Unitas Fratrum, and Cornelius v. Laar, Agent", to James Hutton, authorized him " to empower

Frederic Marshall for to sell etc., parcel
or parcels of Wachovia;" and a second
Power of Attorney from James Hutton
to Marshall, dated October 9th, 1767,
permitted him to sell, convey, etc., lands
in Wachovia, " reserving thereout nevertheless to James Charlesworth, of Pud-
sey, County of York, Great Britain * *
the Usual Quit Rents * * reserved
by grants * * to Granville, which
since the said Earl's death, have been
purchased by the said James Charlesworth, of Robert Earl Granville, his late
Lordship's only son and heir." In 1768,
therefore, Marshall returned to Salem,
as the "Administrator" of the Unity.
Each Congregation also had its "Warden" to attend to its secular affairs, and
each leased from the Unity such lands as
it needed, subleasing them in turn to its
individual members. Thus in 1772 the *Salem Land* was measured, and found to contain 3,159¾ acres, of which 82¼ acres on
the northwest corner were returned to
the Unity in 1786, leaving 3,077½ acres,

paying £69:5:5 rent to the Administration.

In 1771 Wachovia was removed from the care of the Church at Bethlehem, Pa., and was constituted as the Southern Province of the Moravian Church, with full powers for local government.

For two years previous to 1773 the Wachovia Tract lay half in Surry and half in Rowan County. This the inhabitants found very inconvenient, since their interests were all one, and a special Act had made them one Parish, *Dobbs*, although the Parish lines usually coincided with the county lines; the Legislature meeting in March of that year therefore passed an Act changing the Surry line so that it began

"at a point in the line dividing Rowan and Guilford Counties, thirty-six miles from the southeast corner of Rowan, thence running a due west course, to the ridge dividing the waters of the Yadkin and Catawba rivers, which line is to be parallel to Earl Granville's south boundary line (excepting where the bounds of the Parish of Dobbs interfere, which

Parish is hereby intended and declared to be included in Surry county)."

There is a discrepancy of six miles in the distance of the Surry line from Earl Granville's line, as given by the Acts of 1770 and 1773, which is due either to a use of statute miles in the one instance and geographical miles in the other, or to an inaccuracy in the survey. The line itself was changed only at the boundary of Dobbs Parish, where it took the many-angled course which still marks the southern limit of Forsyth County.

CHAPTER III.

WACHOVIA AND THE REVOLUTION-
ARY WAR.

In 1775, Frederick William Marshall went to Europe, to attend a General Synod of the Church, held at Barby, Saxony, and was detained abroad for four years, on account of the Revolutionary War, which broke out in 1776.

The following years were very trying for the Brethren, who, bereft of the counsels of their able leader, were at a loss how to conduct themselves in the changing conditions of the time. Before his departure, already, the trouble had begun, for as they refused to espouse the cause either of Regulator or of royal Governor, both parties regarded them with suspicion, and they were several times called to account for rendering

3

secret aid to the Tories. But each investigation proved them innocent of any departure from their claimed neutrality, and throughout the war they refrained, for conscience' sake, from bearing arms.

In November, 1777, the Legislature, in session at Newbern, passed the so-called "Confiscation Act," which decreed that—

" All the lands * * and movable property within this State * * to which any person had title on the fourth day of July in the year 1776, and who on said day was absent from this State, and every part of the United States, and who is still absent from the same, * * shall, and are hereby declared to be confiscated to the use of this State ; unless such person shall, at the next general assembly which shall be held after the first day of October in the year 1778, appear, and be, by the said assembly, admitted to the privilege of a citizen of this State," etc.

With these conditions the Brethren were unable to comply, for, although James Hutton, on October 28th, 1778, transferred the title to Frederick Marshall (who was a citizen of North Carolina), and appointed Rev. John Michael

Graff, Jacob Blum, Esq., and Traugott Bagge his attorneys to attend to making the transfer secure in America, yet Marshall still remained abroad. The older and more influential members were, moreover, unwilling to take the oath of allegiance to the new government and abjure King George, although many of the younger men did so. One of the Brethren was sent to Bethlehem, Pa., to consult with the Church there, but they were in the same dilemma, and could give no aid. Many people believed that the Moravians would surely be driven out, and entered various parcels of their land, including the towns of Salem and Bethabara and the two mills, rating these more valuable portions at 50 shillings, Continental money, for 100 acres.

The session of the Legislature which ended in January, 1779, passed an Act stating that—

"Whereas, many persons who come within the descriptions of the aforesaid act (Confiscation Act, 1777) * * have failed or neglected to appear before the general Assembly during the 'present session. * * Be it therefore enacted, That all the lands * * of every person and persons who come within the descriptions of the aforesaid act * * shall be forfeited to the State," etc.

This made matters still worse for the Brethren, and gave them no choice as to their future attitude toward the new government. Many of the Brethren opposed the taking of an oath under any circumstances, but this objection was met by the same Legislature in " An act to prescribe the Affirmation of Allegiance and Fidelity to this State to be taken by the Unitas Fratrum or Moravians, Menonites, and Dunkards, and granting them certain indulgencies therein mentioned and other Purposes." The Act read as follows:

"In order to quiet the Consciences and indulge the religious Scruples of the Sects called the Unitas Fratrum or Moravians, Quakers, Menonites, and Dunkards ; *Be it enacted, etc.*, That the Affirmation of Allegiance and Fidelity to this State, shall hereafter be taken by all the above People in the Form following : [Then follows the form.] Which said Affirmation being taken before any Justice of the Peace in the County where they reside, at or before the first day of May next, shall entitle them to all those Rights, Privileges and Immunities they heretofore respectively enjoyed, any law to the contrary notwithstanding, the Assessment and payment of Taxes only accepted."

All the Brethren, therefore, who had not yet taken the Test Oath, now solemnly *affirmed* their fealty to the United States, and their trouble was settled for a time. In the Fall of the year Frederick William Marshall returned from Europe, and was followed in the Spring of 1780 by Bishop J. F. Reichel, who came as the representative of the General Board of the Unitas Fratrum, and, under the direction of these two, the Brethren fell into harmony with the new order of things in their adopted country.

In February, 1781, the British Army, under Lord Cornwallis, traversed the county, camping near Bethabara and passing through Salem, but committing no serious depredations.

A more welcome guest came ten years later, when George Washington, the first

President of the United States, spent a
day in Salem on his way to visit Gov.
Martin. He passed the time inspecting
the various establishments of the Brethren, visited the Brothers' and Sisters'
Houses, and was especially pleased with
the Water-works. In the evening " six
Brethren dined with him, and at night
the President, his Secretary, and Gov.
Martin of North Carolina, who had come
to meet him, attended the singing meeting to their great edification."

In November, 1781, sixty-three members of the Assembly, with Governor
Alexander Martin, met in Salem, but
failed to hold their session through lack
of a quorum. The visit was repeated in
January, 1782, and was of much value
to the Brethren, as through its represen-
tatives the State learned to know and
better understand their real intentions,
and the more readily decided in their
favor the disputed title to the Wachovia
Tract.

Although the Brethren had been unmo-

lested since taking the Affirmation of
Allegiance to the American Government,
many persons contended that Frederick
William Marshall had no legal right to
the title, since through the Confiscation
Act James Hutton, an alien, had lost all
claim to it *before* going through the form
of transferring it to Marshall. But when
the deeds were first made to Hutton,
Count Zinzendorf had insisted upon the
insertion of the clause "in trust for the
Unitas Fratrum," and while the nominal
owner had not been a citizen of Carolina
when he transferred the title, those for
whom he held the land "in trust" had
been resident in the State for many years,
and could not justly be dispossessed.
The Legislature, therefore, relinquishing
any claim it might have had, passed an
Act on April 13th, 1782, "To vest in
Frederick William Marshall, Esquire, of
Salem, in Surry County, all the lands of
the Unitas Fratrum, in this state, for the
use of the United Brethren."

CHAPTER IV.

THE TITLE TO WACHOVIA.

The Act, vesting the title to the lands of the Unitas Fratrum (in N. C.) in Fred. Wm. Marshall, read as follows:

"1. Whereas, Frederick William Marshall, esquire, of Salem in Surry county, hath made it appear to this General Assembly that all the tracts of land in this state belonging to the lord advocate, the chancellor and the agent of the Unitas Fratrum, or united brethren, have been transferred to him from the former possessors, in trust for the Unitas Fratrum, or united brethren; and whereas doubts have arisen whether the said tracts do not come within the description of the confiscation act; and to quiet the minds of those to whom conveyances have been, or are to be made, of any part or parts thereof; II. *Be it therefore enacted, by the General Assembly of the state of North Carolina, and it is hereby enacted by authority of the same,* that a certain deed of lease and release, dated the twenty-seventh and twenty eighth of October, one thousand

seven hundred and seventy-eight, from James
Hutton, conveying the tract of Wachovia, in
Surry county, to said Frederick William Marshall, be hereby declared valid in law, and to
be admitted to probate in the county of Surry,
and registered in the register's office thereof,
agreeable to the testimonials thereunto apper-
taining; and that all lands which by deed of
bargain and sale of the twentieth of April, one
thousand seven hundred and sixty-four,
between William Churton and Charles Metcalf, registered in the county of Orange in
book number one, page one hundred and six,
and in Rowan county, in book E, number five,
page four hundred and fifty-two, &c., were
then conveyed to said Charles Metcalf, be
hereby vested in the said Frederick William
Marshall in trust as aforesaid; and all conveyances of the above mentioned lands, or any of
them, made, or which shall be made by the
said Frederick William Marshall, shall be as
good and valid to all intents and purposes as
if the confiscation act had never passed.

III. *And be it further enacted by the authority aforesaid*, that the power of Attorney of
Christian Frederick Cossart, dated the third
of November, one thousand seven hundred
and seventy-two, empowering said Frederick
William Marshall to sell his lands, be admitted
to probate and registry in the county of
Wilkes, and be as good and valid in law as it
could or might have been, had the act of confiscation never passed."

The "Wachovia Tract" referred to in this Act, was, of course, that purchased from Lord Granville at the beginning of the Moravian settlement in Carolina.

The "Metcalf Lands" consisted of between eleven and twelve thousand acres, granted by Earl Granville to Wm. Churton, his surveyor-general, on Jan. 5th, 1762, and surveyed in twenty tracts by Churton himself, Jacob Lash of Wachovia, and Thos. Child of Suffolk, Va.

On April 20th, 1764, Wm. Churton sold these tracts to Charles Metcalf, the deed mentioning 20£ consideration. Charles Metcalf, in turn, sold lots 18, 19 and 20 to his sister Mary. February 6, 1772, Chas. Metcalf sent a Power of Attorney to F. W. Marshall to sell his land, and on Jan. 14, 1773, "Mary Metcalf of Chelsea in the county of Middlesex," gave similar authority to Marshall concerning her share. Marshall decided to buy the lands for the Unitas Fratrum, and therefore, on October 21st, 1778, Power of Attorney was sent by Metcalf and his sister to Rev. Michael Graff, Jacob Bonn and Traugott Bagge to sell the 17 tracts for 200£. and the 3 tracts for 50£.

The 20 Metcalf tracts were not together like the Wachovia Tract, but were scattered along the water-courses in what were then Rowan and Orange Counties. Several formed the Blanket Bottom tract, on the creek of that name; others were on the branches of Abbott's Creek, Muddy Creek, etc., and still others in what are now Person and Caswell Counties.

During all these years the Unity had been steadily paying an annual quit-rent to the heir of Lord Granville and those to whom he afterward sold it. In 1788 the Rev. Wm. Horne, "late of Dublin but now of Ballondary in the County of Antrim in the Kingdom of Ireland," was "Lord of the Fee," and from him, on May 5th, F. W. Marshall bought for 5 shillings, "all and every of 19 several and distinct annual Rents stipulated provided reserved

and mentioned in and by 19 several Indentures
or Grants * * made between John Earl
Granville of the one part and James Hutton
of the other part, * * making in the whole
the Annual Sum of £148:9:2½ Sterling Money of
Great Britain."

This was only a legal preliminary to
the transaction of the following day,
May 6th, when Marshall, as agent for
the Unitas Fratrum, received the fee
simple title to the Wachovia Tract, paying £1,000 for it. Rev. Daniel Koehler,
Rev. Christian Benzien, and Traugott
Bagge were appointed by Horne as his
attorneys to have the deed registered in
North Carolina.

The actual purchase price of Wachovia
may therefore be estimated thus:

Purchase money	£ 500:	$ 2,420 00
4 per cent. interest. 4 yrs,	£ 80:	387 20
Quit-rent, 35 years,	£5192:2:3	25,129 82
Purchase of Title,	£1000:	4,840 00
	£6772:2:3	$32,777 02

On Feb. 11th, 1802, F. W. Marshall
died, and by his will Christian Lewis
Benzien became "Proprietor," holding
the title to the lands of the Unitas Fra-

trum in N. C. Sometimes the "Proprietor" also held the position of "Administrator," or agent of the Unity in the management of its local business affairs, at other times the offices were separate. The Proprietors of the Wachovia Tract, etc., were :

1. James Hutton, of London, Aug. 7th, 1753—Oct. 28th. 1778 ;
   Title transferred by deed to
2. Frederick William Marshall, of Salem, N. C., 1778—Feb. 11th, 1802 ;
   Transferred by will to
3. Christian Lewis Benzien, of Salem, 1802—November 13th, 1811 ;
   Transferred by will to
4. John Gebhard Cunow, of Bethlehem, Pa., 1811—March 28, 1822 ;
   Transferred by deed to
5. Lewis David von Schweinitz, of Bethlehem, Pa., 1822 — February 8th, 1834 ;
   Transferred by will to
6. William Henry Van Vleck, of New York City, 1834—August 7th, 1844;
   Transferred by deed to

7. Charles F. Kluge, of Salem, N. C.,
    1844—April 19th, 1853;
        Transferred by deed to
8. Emil A. de Schweinitz, of Salem,
    1853—December 1st, 1877:
        Transferred by deed to
9. The Board of Provincial Elders of the
    Southern Province of the Moravian
    Church.

The Administrators of the Southern
Province during the same years were:

1. Frederick William Marshall, 1763—
    1802;
2. Christian Lewis Benzien, 1802—1811;
3. Lewis David von Schweinitz, 1812—
    1821;
4. Theodore Shultz, 1821—1844;
5. Charles F. Kluge, 1844—1853;
6. Emil A. de Schweinitz, 1853—1877.

The transfer of title to the Board of
Provincial Elders was accompanied by
an actual purchase of the property
involved, and by it both the Proprietor-
ship and the Administration came to an
end.

CHAPTER V.

KERNERSVILLE, FRIEDBERG, FRIEDLAND, HOPE.

About the time that Salem was established in the centre of the Wachovia Tract, several other towns sprang up near the borders of what was to be Forsyth County.

Kernersville, the largest of these, was not originally laid out as a town, but grew gradually to such a size. About 1756 or 1760, Caleb Story, a native of Ireland, bought 400 acres of land, about 12 miles east of Salem, near the Guilford County line. Tradition says he paid for it with 4 gallons of rum. This tract he sold to a certain Dobson, and from this the place came to be called "*Dobson's Cross Roads*," a name it retained for many years.

Mr. Dobson sold the 400 acres to Gottlieb Shober, of Salem, who sold it, in 1817, to Joseph Kerner, a German by birth, but then living near Friedland. During the succeeding years Kerner bought more land in the neighborhood, and at his death, in 1830, left 1100 acres to be divided between his three heirs. Of these, John F. received the portion to the west of what is now Main Street; Phillip took the homestead, and the land to the east, and the daughter, Salome, who had married Appolis Harmon, had a share to the south. In the course of time, a thriving town grew up, some of the land being sold to new settlers, the rest remaining with the branches of the Kerner family; and, in 1869, *Kernersville* was incorporated, and Joseph Armfield was elected the first Mayor.

Friedberg, on the lower edge of the county, had a similar small beginning. In August, 1754, Adam Spach, a native of Pfaffenheim, Alsace, settled about three miles south of the Wachovia line.

He speedily made the acquaintance of the Moravians, taking refuge at Bethabara during the Indian War, and after wards urging the Brethren to come and hold services at his home. This was done, at intervals, until 1766, and meanwhile several families from Pennsylvania had settled in the neighborhood.

Then the church authorities at Salem set apart some 34 acres near the southern boundary of Wachovia for the use of the new congregation, adding to them 77 acres, across the line, bought from Adam Spach. Part of the 77 acres was afterwards sold or exchanged, but the Friedberg Church Land is still divided by the county line.

In 1773, about 81 acres in the neighborhood were purchased for the purpose of building a schoolhouse thereon; this tract was resold at a later time.

The first meeting-house of the Friedberg Congregation was consecrated on March 11th, 1769; Rev. L. G. Bachoff becoming their first resident minister on
4

February 18th, 1770. In January, 1772,
" the Friedberg Congregation of the
Unitas Fratrum " was formally established ; and on February 19th, 1786, the
corner-stone was laid for a larger church,
which was consecrated May 12th, 1788,
and served until 1827, when the present
church was built.

The settlement at *Friedland*, near the
eastern line of the Wachovia survey, was
begun in a different manner.

In 1769 six German families arrived
in Wachovia. They were part of a company of emigrants from the Palatinate
and Wurtemburg, who, about 1738, had
settled near Broad Bay, in Maine. There
they became acquainted with one of the
Moravian Brethren, and wished to establish a congregation, but there were legal
difficulties concerning their title deeds,
so they resolved to move to North Carolina. Having been shipwrecked on the
coast of Virginia, they came by way of
Wilmington, and arrived in Wachovia,
poor, wayworn, and many of them in ill

health. They were given temporary
homes in Bethabara and Salem, and the
next year were joined by eight more
families. As they did not wish to remain
in Salem, 1,800 acres of the Unity's land
were sold to them, the Administration
reserving 30 acres in the center of the
tract for a church and school-house. In
February, 1772, the corner-stone of the
church was laid, the building was consecrated on February 18th, 1775, with
Rev. Tycho Nissen as the first pastor,
and the "Friendland Congregation"
was formally recognized in September,
1780.

The first English congregation in Wachovia was *Hope*, in the southwestern
corner of the tract. Several settlers in
that quarter had enjoyed the protection
of the "Dutch Fort" during the Indian
War, and had afterward joined the congregation at Friedberg; but that was
purely German, and they desired an
English-speaking church of their own.
Meetings had been held for them as early

as 1758; and in 1775—several English
families from Carrol's Manor, Maryland,
and elsewhere, having located in that
section of Wachovia—a church was
begun, which was consecrated March
28th, 1780; and Rev. John Christian
Fritz was placed in charge of the little
company which was, on the 28th of August, fully constituted a congregation of
the Brethren's Church. The burial
ground was laid out during the same
year.

CHAPTER VI.

THE COURT HOUSE TRACT.

In January, 1849, as has been already stated, the Legislature of North Carolina divided the County of Stokes into two parts, *Stokes* and *Forsyth*, and appointed five Commissioners for each of the counties. The first duty of these Commissioners was to select and purchase the site for the Court House and other public buildings. This created a great deal of discussion, for as Salem lay almost in the center of Forsyth, it seemed necessary to choose land in that neighborhood for the county town.

The Commissioners applied to the *Aufseher Collegium* of the Salem Congregation for some 31 acres of land, north of the town, but they refused to decide so weighty a question, and referred the

matter to the *Gemeinrath*, or Congregation Council. Then the debate waxed
warm. A new town would spring up,
new settlers would come in, their views
would conflict with those of the Brethren, Moravian rules and ways would be
disturbed, perhaps destroyed—so said
the conservative element, and wished to
keep the Court House as far away as
possible; while the progressive party
thought the new settlers would give new
life to the community, and that, if the
new town was brought near Salem, the
disturbing features would adjust themselves.

The Congregation Council, held February 5th, 1849, agreed to sell 31 acres
to the Commissioners, the southern line to
come no nearer Salem than the northern
side of the lot held under lease by Mr.
Thos. J. Wilson [now the Hanes House].
In March, further conditions were made
that the Court House should be in the
centre of the tract, and the new streets
should be continuations of those in

Salem ; and the price was fixed at $5.00 an acre, the same amount that the Administrator was getting for land sold in the vicinity. The Congregation Council met again on the 10th of April, and by a vote of 59 to 9 authorized the *Aufseher Collegium* to sell 50 or 51 acres to the Commissioners, the line to be moved further south [to the present line], and therefore nearer Salem.

The Commissioners were requested to build the Court House on a knoll a little north of Mr. Wilson's, and agreed to do so, and the plan for the future town was decided upon. The minority then withdrew their objections, and the vote of the Council was made unanimous. On the 12th of May, 1849, Charles F. Kluge, Proprietor and Administrator, gave a deed for 51¼ acres of Salem Land to the Commissioners of Forsyth County.

The deed to the land for the Forsyth Court House read as follows :

" Whereas the General Assembly of N. C. did at its last Session pass an act to divide the County of Stokes into two distinct Counties,

and another supplemental thereto, and in said
Act appoint 5 Commissioners to select a site
for the erection of the public buildings of Forsythe Co. purchase land for the purpose, lay
off and sell town lots and so forth; and whereas
said Commissioners have applied to me Charles
F. Kluge of the County of Forsythe and State
of N. C. for a tract of land adjoining the town
of Salem, on which to erect said buildings, I
have agreed to sell to them, or as the said Act
requires to the Chairman of the County Court,
the desired tract of land on the following conditions; to wit : that said Chairman as soon
as required to do so by the parties interested
do make a deed in fee to the School Committee of the district including the town of Salem,
for the lot on which the public schoolhouse
now stands and marked No. 1 on the appended
plot, which lot is to be used as a public school
lot , and further do make a deed in fee simple
to Thos. J. Wilson for the lot on which he
now lives, being lot No. 45 on the appended
plot, said Wilson paying a reasonable and
moderate price for the same, which is to be
paid one half to said Chairman and one half
to me Charles F. Kluge. Therefore

" This Indenture witnesseth that I Charles
F. Kluge of said County and State have bar-
gained and sold, and by these presents do bargain and sell in consideration of the above
agreement and further in consideration of the
Sum of Two hundred and fifty-six and one
quarter Dollars secured to me this day by a

bond given by Fr. Fries Chairman of the
County Court of Forsythe Co. unto said Francis Fries Chairman as aforesaid and his successors forever, all that tract or parcel of land
situate lying and being in the Co. of Forsythe
State of N. C. and adjoining the town of Salem or rather being a part thereof, Beginning
at a Stake the South East Corner of said tract,
running North 10° West 41 poles and 21 links
to a Stake, thence North $8\frac{1}{2}$° West 110 poles
and 9 links to a Stone, thence South $81\frac{1}{2}$° West
13 poles and 20 links to a Stone, thence North
$8\frac{1}{2}$° West 28 poles and 10 links to a Stake in the
Salem town line, thence along said line South
88° West 33 poles and 5 links to a Stake in V.
Zevely's line, thence South $8\frac{1}{2}$° East 143 poles
and 20 links to a Stake, South 10° East 41 poles
and 21 links to a Stake, thence North 80° East
47 poles and 4 links to the Beginning. Containing $51\frac{1}{4}$ acres, more or less.

"To have and to hold unto the said Francis
Fries Chairman as aforesaid and his Successors for the purposes herein before stated and
as set forth in the Act of the General Assembly as first above mentioned.

"And I do further promise forever to war-
rent and defend the title of the above tract of
land unto the said F. Fries Chairman as aforesaid and his Successors against the Claim or
Claims of all and every other person or persons whatsoever.

"In witness whereof I Charles F. Kluge do

hereunto set my hand and affix my Seal this twelfth, day of May in the year of our Lord One thousand eight hundred and forty-nine.

CHARLES F. KLUGE."

F. C. MEINUNG.
S. THOS. PFOHL.

Although the deed to the Forsyth Commissioners was made by Charles F. Kluge, the Administrator of the Unity, the land was really owned by the Salem Congregation. " In 1771 *Salem Congregation Diacony*, or that financial Institution, from the procceds of which the congregation at Salem was to be maintained as a Moravian congregation, was established. The Diacony assumed all the liabilities incurred in the erection of buildings in Salem, and a tract of land originally containing 3,159 Acres was granted to it, under lease, for a fixed annual rent." At first this annual rent was £69:5:5, equal to $335.26, about 10½c per acre, but some of the land was sold, and the annual rent decreased, and in 1826 the Salem Diacony held 2,485 acres, paying $143.77½, or about 6c. per acre.

In 1826 this lease was determined, and the tract was sold to the Salem Congregation Diacony for $2,795.62½, or $1.12½ per acre. This amount was paid off gradually, the last payment being made in April, 1849, by part of the purchase money of the Court House Tract. But the title could not be transferred to the Salem Diacony because that was not a corporate body, and one condition of the sale was that "the legal title was to remain in the Proprietor." Therefore the deed to the Court House Tract was given by Chas. F. Kluge, then Proprietor of Wachovia as well as Administrator.

In the course of time it became evident that the lease system—under which no one could own, and only members of the Moravian Church could lease houses in Salem—was no longer advantageous; and as the purchase of the "Salem Land" had made it no longer a necessity, the Congregation Council of November 17th, 1856, abolished it as the unvarying rule, although members who desired might continue to hold their property in that manner.

In January, 1874, the General Assembly of North Carolina enacted—

"That the members of the Congregation of United Brethren, commonly called Moravians, of the town of Salem and its vicinity, be, and the same are hereby created and erected into one body politic and corporate in deed and in law, by the name, style and title of ' *The Congregation of United Brethren of Salem and its vicinity ;*' "

and on July 10th, 1874, Emil A. de Schweinitz, then Proprietor, tranferred to it the fee simple title to the remaining Salem Land, the Church and Academy property alone excepted.

The rest of the Moravian lands in North Carolina remained in the hands of the Unity for several years more. In 1771 the Wachovia Sustentation Diacony was established. While the Salem Congregation Diacony concerned itself with the affairs of the Salem Congregation, this Diacony cared for the finances for the general work of the Church in the Southern Province. During the succeeding years the proceeds from the store at Bethabara, and several trades carried on there, furnished revenue enough ; but as expenses increased, even with the aid of contributions from various sources, the Wachovia Sustentation Diacony found difficulty in raising the necessary funds, and finally became deeply indebted to the Administrator in Wachovia. This debt was canceled by returning to the Unity certain lands which had been set apart for this Diacony.

The General Synod, which met in Herrnhut, Germany, in 1857, decided to divide among the Provinces certain funds then in hand, and the share of the Southern Province put the Wachovia Sustentation Diacony on a comfortable footing again. The business of the Wachovia Sustentation Diacony was in the hands of " *The Board of Provincial Elders of the Southern Province of the Moravian Church or Unitas Fratrum*," and in January, 1877, this Board was incorporated.

In December, 1877, the Provincial

Elders' Conference purchased from the Unity all the land in the Southern Province still belonging to the general Board of the Unitas Fratrum, paying for it the sum of $43,472.57, about $12,000 cash down, and the rest in annual instalments, the last payment being made in November, 1886. The deed from the Unity to the Provincial Elders' Conference was made December 1st, 1877.

The plan for the new Court House Town, as suggested by the Commissioners and approved by the Salem Congregation Council, consisted of 71 lots, exclusive of the Court House Square. These were included between what are now known as Church Street and Trade Street (which then began at the Salem line) as far north as Sixth Street, and between Main and Trade Streets to Seventh Street.

Of these lots, as already stated, Mr. Thos. J. Wilson held No. 45 under lease from the Salem Congregation, and No. 1 was reserved for the Public School; the rest were sold at auction, the first sale being held May 12th, 1849. The terms offered were: " A credit of one and two years, the purchaser securing the amount of his bid by an approved bond, and title in fee simple to be made as soon as the purchase money shall have been paid." The first purchaser was Robert Gray, who bought Lot No. 41 (the Wachovia National Bank corner) for $465.00. This was the highest price paid, the sums ranging from this to $46.00 for the lot next the School House. All the lots south of Fourth Street, and five above it, were sold at this time, and aggregated $6,712.25.

June 22d, 1849, a second sale was made, and the remaining lots were sold at prices from $35.00 to $170.00, five lots being reserved for the jail and other purposes, so that with one or two additional transactions the total receipts from the sale of the lots were $8,833.50.

On June 20th, 1849, the County Court appropriated $9,000.00 to the building

of a Court House and Jail.   In September they ordered " that Thos. J. Wilson
and C. L. Banner be appointed Commissioners to have the streets on the site of
the new Court House cleaned out on the
best terms they can, and to make such
contracts and regulations for the same
as they may deem to the best interest of
Forsyth Co.," and in December Darius
H. Starbuck was added to the Committee.   At the latter term there were
opened as Public Highways " one road
to lead from the location of the Court
House, west, to intersect the Shallowford
road at the top of Atwood's Hill, not far
from the corner of Wm. Fries' field,"
and " one other road from the said location of the Court House to intersect the
Belew's Creek road in a South-east direction from said location."   It was like-
wise ordered "that the new Main and
Cross streets lately laid out at the location of the Court House in Salem, be
viewed and made Public Highways
according to law."

On March 18th, 1850, the Commissioners appointed by the Legislature were authorized to " proceed to take into their possession the bonds and debts due or hereafter to become due for the lots, and pay over the proceeds to those with whom they may have contracted in the erection of the Public Buildings and for other necessary expenses."

In September Thos. J. Wilson and F. L. Gorrel were appointed Commissioners " to have a suitable enclosure put around the Court House, 200 feet square, and to have the trees in said Square trimmed and topped." The fence was to be made " of good sawed white or post Oak posts and plank 4 or 5 inches wide, to be dressed and nailed to the posts and painted, provided the Committee think that they can have the work done at a moderate price."

In September, 1849, it was ordered by the Court that F. C. Meinung, Michael Hauser and Matthew Crews, who had been Wardens of the Poor for Forsyth County while it was still a part of Stokes,

5

should continue to act in that capacity, and should associate with themselves as many others as the law required, to hold office until the regular election in March. In December, F. C. Meinung, C. L. Banner and Michael Hauser were appointed a Committee to select a site for a Poor House, and in March, 1850, they were empowered to buy land and proceed with the building.

The tract selected contained about 90 acres, lying " on Waters of Brushy Fork, Middle Fork of Muddy Creek, and on both sides of the road leading to Germanton," and was about three and a half miles northeast of the Court House. On May 1st, 1850, it was bought for $270.00 from Chas. F. Kluge, the Administrator of the Unity in Wachovia; the deed was probated in 1852 at the March term of Court. In order to obtain funds for buying the land and for necessary buildings the Court, in June, 1850, authorized the Committee to borrow $1,000.00, which the County of Forsyth pledged itself to repay.

CHAPTER VII.

NAMING THE COUNTY TOWN.

Up to this time the new County Town
had possessed no separate name, and
there was much difference of opinion as
to what it should be. In the Court of
Pleas and Quarter Sessions, on June
17th, 1850, an attempt was made to have
it settled by a vote of the people, and
the motion is recorded in full in the Min-
utes, as follows :

" Whereas in the supplemental act of the
last General Assembly dividing the County of
Stokes there was no name given nor any way
pointed out by which a name should be given
the County Seat of Forsyth County: And
whereas the Commissioners of said County
having located the County Seat and Public
Buildings immediately adjoining the Town of
Salem (and some of its citizens having since
built to an adjoining lot of the Court House
Tract) it was believed by the Committee, or a
majority of them, that it was unnecessary to

give the County Seat of Forsyth County any
other name than *Salem*, and so sold the lots
and have made deeds under that name:

" And whereas of late it appears that the
name of Salem for the County Seat of Forsyth
has given a good deal of dissatisfaction to the
people in some portions of the County, and as
the Courts of said County will be, in a few
months, held at the new Court House, it is
necessary that the said Court House should
have a permanent name to which process
should be returned:

" And whereas this Court believing that as
no provision has been made by the Legislature for a name, and also believing that a
majority of the people may legally and prop-
erly give the name: It is therefore ordered by
the Court that the Sheriff of Forsyth County
hold an election in said County on the first day
of August next for that purpose, and that the
Judges of the Sheriff's election receive the
votes for the name, and that the name receiving the greatest number of votes be declared
the name of the Court House of Forsyth
County."

But the motion to name the new
Court House Town by a popular vote
having been lost, the matter rested until
the following session of the Legislature,
when Col. Henry Marshall, from near
Salem Chapel, introduced a Bill, and an

Act was passed, "giving a name to the
county town of Forsyth county, and for
other purposes." This Act, which was
ratified January 15th, 1851, read thus:

"Sec. 1. Be it enacted by the General Assembly of the State of N. C. and it is hereby
enacted by the authority of the same, That
hereafter the county town of Forsyth county
shall be styled and known by the name of
Winston."

The name appears for the first time in
the County Records on March 17th, 1851,
when Court was " opened and held at
the Court House in the town of Winston."

Winston was named in honor of Major
Joseph Winston, a prominent North
Carolinian during Revolutionary days.
He was of English ancestry, and was
born in Louisa Co., Va., June 17th, 1746.
Having received a fair education, he, at
the age of seventeen, joined a company
of rangers, and had several encounters
with hostile Indians. In one of these,
the rangers fell into an ambuscade and
were completely routed. Winston was

twice wounded, but made his escape, and
was carried on a comrade's back for three
days, until they reached a frontier cabin.
In 1766 he moved to Surry Co., N. C.,
and settled near Germanton. In 1775
he was a member of the Hillsboro Con-
vention, and was made 2d Major of the
Surry County Militia. The next year
he became ranger of Surry County, and
1st Major of Militia, and served against
the Scotch Tories and the Cherokees. In
1777 he was a member of the Legislature, and, with Waighstill Avery, Wm.
Harper and Robert Lanier, was commis-
sioned by Gov. Caswell to treat with the
Indians, the result being that lands in
North Carolina and Virginia were ceded
to those States. At the battle of King's
Mountain, October 7th, 1780, Major
Winston and his men from Surry and
Wilkes led the right wing of the little
army, and formed the north-eastern section of the circle that closed in, crushed
Ferguson and his British troops, and
began the victory which was completed

at Yorktown. For his services on that day the Legislature afterwards presented him with a sword. Having defeated a band of loyalists in a running fight in February, 1781, he took part in the battle of Guilford Court House in March. Major Winston represented Surry County in the State Senate for three terms, and when Stokes County was formed became the first Senator from that county, serving five times between 1790 and 1812. In 1793–'95, and again in 1803–'7, he was a member of Congress. He died near Germanton, April 21st, 1815.

CHAPTER VIII.

FORSYTH COUNTY COURTS.

Until the Winston Court House could be built, the Forsyth Courts were held in the Concert Hall in Salem, the church authorities having given their permission on condition that no whipping post should be put up there. The appointments of the Hall were very primitive, as appears from an order to the Sheriff to " let out to the lowest bidder on Saturday next the furnishing of sawdust, candles, etc., for the Court at the Town Hall in Salem, at so much per Court," but it answered every purpose for the time being.

" The Act supplemental to an Act to divide the County of Stokes into two distinct Counties " provided that all Justices of the Peace and County Officials

should serve out their terms of office in
the counties in which they lived, the
gaps made by this division to be filled by
appointment of the Court of Pleas and
Quarter Sessions at its first meeting,
those so appointed to hold office until
the annual election.

On March 19th, 1849, sixteen " Gen-
tlemen Justices, appointed and commis-
sioned by the Governor of the State,"
met in the Salem Concert Hall, and took
the several oaths of office.   They then
elected for the ensuing year—

Sheriff—Wm. Flynt,

Clerk of the Court—Andrew J. Stafford,

County Attorney—Thos. J. Wilson,

Register of Deeds—F. C. Meinung,

County Trustee—Geo. Linville,

Coroner—John H. White,

Standard Keeper—Abraham Steiner.

All of the Justices of the Peace were
entitled to sit in the Court of Pleas and
Quarter Sessions, which not only attended
to the affairs of the county, but tried

minor civil and criminal cases, but the
law provided that, if they wished, the
Justices might annually elect a chairman
and several members who should consti-
tute a Special Court, holding the Court
of Pleas and Quarter Sessions on the
third Monday in March, June, September and December.

On March 20th, therefore, the Justices
elected as the Special Court—

Francis Fries, Chairman.
Philip Barrow,
Andrew M. Gamble,
John Reich,
Jesse A. Waugh.

The Finance Committee consisted of—

C. L. Banner,
Israel G. Lash,
Francis Fries.

The members of the Special Court
were each allowed $1.50 per day while
in session, and the Finance Committee
the same for such time as was needed for
their official duties. The county taxes
were ordered thus:

County tax, 60c. poll,19c. per $100.00 real estate.
Poor tax, 24¾ " 5¾ " " " "
School tax, 15 " 7½ " " " "

Total, 99¾c. p'l,32¼c. per $100.00 real est.

The Superior Court and a Court of
Equity met twice a year, on the second
Monday after the fourth Monday in
March and September, the first Judge
presiding in Forsyth being John M.
Dick.

The first case of any interest was tried
in October, 1850, before Judge Mathias
E. Manly, Adam Crooks and Jesse Mc-
Bride being indicted for circulating lit-
erature inciting the negro slaves to
rebellion. Crooks was found "not guilty"
in the particular instance selected for
trial, but McBride was sentenced to be
imprisoned one year, stand in the pillory
one hour, and receive twenty lashes. He
appealed to the Supreme Court, giving
bond for $1,000.00, and ran away before
getting a new trial.

In April, 1851, the Superior Court
was held in the new Court House in

Winston, Judge J. L. Baily presiding. During this term Edmund Martin, a free negro, accused of stealing a slave, was condemned to death; but having appealed to the Supreme Court, he was granted a new trial, and was acquitted.

The first execution ordered by a Forsyth Court took place in November, 1852, when Charles, a slave, the property of W. J. McElroy, was hanged for murder, having been convicted in October of that year.

In March, 1850, C. L. Banner was elected chairman of the Court of Pleas and Quarter Sessions.

The Minute Docket of that Court, under date of December 16th, 1850, contains an account of the opening of the new Court House:

"On motion it was resolved that the Court adjourn to meet again at 1 o'clock P. M. at the new Court House, the fact having been ascertained that said building was in sufficient state of preparation for the Sessions of the Court to be held therein." "Court met agreeably to adjournment. Present, C. L. Banner, John Butner, Caleb H. Matthews, H. R. Lehman.

FIRST COURT HOUSE.

After the singing of a hymn, the Rev. Michael
Doub delivered a prayer to Almighty God,
that whatever might be transacted within the
walls of this building might tend to the prop-
agation of Justice, and the promotion of mor-
ality and Religion. On motion it was ordered
by the Court that ministers of the Gospel of
all respectable denominations be permitted to
preach in the Court House; and that the person for the time having the care and custody
of the Court House is hereby directed to hand
over the keys to any one calling for them for
the purpose aforesaid. Provided, however,
that the license shall not be so construed as to
include the denomination called the 'True
Wesleyans.' "

The Court House, so auspiciously
opened, was a two story brick building,
44x60 feet, standing with its gable end
fronting the south. The portico, 12 feet
wide, stretched across the entire front,
the roof being supported by four large
pillars, each 30 feet high. In the vesti-
bule, stairways on the right and left led
to the second floor, which was devoted
to the Court Room. The first story had
a corridor running from south to north,
with three rooms on each side, the north-
west room being occupied by the Clerk

of the Court, while the Register of Deeds
had the north-east, the Sheriff the middle, and the Grand Jury the south-east
room. This left two vacant rooms,
which were rented as lawyers' offices,
until the south-west one was taken for
the County Board of Education, and the
middle west became a store room. Later,
the partition between the store room and
Clerk of the Court's office was torn away
to give the Clerk more place.; the Sheriff
took the south-west room, and the retir-
ing Sheriff used the middle east until his
business was completed. The petit jury
had no place assigned, but met in which-
ever room was convenient, and in fine
weather out under the trees.

A memorandum is still preserved,
showing the cost of the buildings and
how this cost was met:

		$	c.
DEBIT.			
Cost of Buildings, etc.—			
Brick, lumber	$4284	53	
Carpenters' work	1752	36	
Brick laying and plaster'g,	1023	80	
Digging, glazing, iron work, etc	1778	90	
		8839	59

Court House Well.. 42 23
Discount on Cash payment for Lots........ 90 56
Interest on money advanced by F. Fries 48 00
Interest on money borrowed...................... 63 00
                                                            ————
                                                            $9083 38

CREDIT. $ c.
Sale of Lots—1st Sale................$6712 25
             2d   " 2021 75
             Additional.......... 99 50
                                   ———— 8833 50
Interest on time payments on Lots...... 136 64
Deducted from cost of Buildings........... 10 00
     Balance to be paid by the Co. Treas. 103 24
                                                            ————
                                                            $9083 38

With the $256.25, the amount paid for
the land for the County Town, the Court
House site and building really cost the
County just $359.49.

Having entered into possession of its
new quarters, the Court authorized Francis Fries to purchase a bell, weighing
about 300 pounds, and have it hung in
the Court House cupola; desired the
building Commissioners to have light-
ning rods put on the Court House and
Jail, and a ball and vane affixed to the
rod above the cupola on the Court House;

and appointed C. L. Banner to superintend the construction of suitable shelves for the use of the Clerks of the County and Superior Courts.

March 17th, 1851, Court was "opened and held at the Court House in *Winston*," and payment made for the temporary meeting place in Salem, $50.00 being allowed for the Concert Hall, and $22.00 for a Grand Jury Room in Mr. James Hall's house. The Sheriff was ordered to "procure a carpet to cover the floor of the Court Room on the most reasonable terms, said carpet within the Bar to be Store Carpet, and without the Bar home-made." He was also "to let the keeping of the Court House to the lowest bidder on Saturday of each March Court," the contractor to see that the building and Square were kept in good condition, rooms, hall and stairs dusted during Court week, and candles and wood furnished when needed. The keys were left with the Clerk of the County Court.

The Court of Pleas and Quarter Sessions continued to meet until the upheaval and reconstruction of 1868, when it was abolished by the new Constitution, the government of county affairs being vested in the Board of County Commissioners, and the judicial functions reverting to the Superior Court.

In 1877 a Court " inferior to the Superior Court " was established in Forsyth, for the trial of criminal actions. It was held by three men chosen by the Justices of the Peace from the body of the county, and they, in their turn, elected one of their number as Presiding Justice. The Inferior Courts continued to be held until 1885, when they were abolished, all cases being transferred to the Superior Court.

CHAPTER IX.

COUNTY MILITIA.

The breaking out of the Civil War, and the reconstruction following those troubled years, brought various other changes into the county. The first of these was the crumbling of the old system of County Militia, which had originally been a necessity for the protection of the settlement, but had grown weak and formal during many years of purely nominal service, and was discarded in the face of active warfare.

The Lords Proprietors of Carolina saw the needs that might arise during the early years of that province, and secured provision for them in the Charter granted them by Charles I.

" And because that in so remote a country, and scituate among so many barbarous nations, and the invasions as well of salvages as

of other enemies, pirates and robbers, may
probably be feared ; therefore we have given
and do give power unto the said Edward, Earl
of Clarendon, etc., by themselves, or their
captains, or other their officers, to levy, mus-
ter and train all sorts of men of what condition or wheresoever born, in the said province
for the time being, and make war, and pursue
the enemies aforesaid."

The Militia was therefore organized
throughout the colony, new companies
being formed as the settlements extended,
the enrollment including all able-bodied
men between the ages of eighteen and
forty-five. It did efficient work during
the trouble with the Indians, and in the
Revolutionary War was the main defense
of North Carolina against the invasions
of Lord Cornwallis, her regulars having
been taken prisoners at the fall of
Charleston. More than 5,000 of the
North Carolina Militia were sent to help
the South Carolinians in their futile
attempt to beat back the British troops ;
and when, flushed with conquest, Cornwallis thought to crush North Carolina
also, he found himself in " a nest of hor-

nets," harrassed by the Militia, who time
and again cut off portions of his army,
until the disillusioned General was forced
to beat a retreat.

Most unfortunately the army registers
do not contain the names of any of the
volunteer troops or Militia, and as the
latter were called out in detachments,
usually to serve a three months' " tour,"
and then disband, it is impossible to fol-
low with accuracy the companies raised
in any locality.

The victory at King's Mountain was
won by volunteers from among the Militia of the western part of the State, and
into this battle Major Joseph Winston
led a body of men from Surry County,
among them being Henry Grieger, of the
north-western portion of what is now
Forsyth. No doubt family tradition pre-
serves the names of many other patriots
who shared in that fierce, decisive
engagement, and it is to be hoped that
they will yet be placed on the honor roll
of history.

In 1781, General William Lee Davidson called out a detachment of Militia
from the Salisbury and Morganton Districts (which included the Muddy Creek
regions), and they helped defend the
fords of the Catawba against Cornwallis,
and about the middle of February, under
command of Gen. Andrew Pickens,
passed through Salem on their way to
the short but fierce campaign which preceded the battle of Guilford Court House,
fought on March 15th, 1781. Pickens'
command was not in that engagement,
for their time was up, and they had disbanded; but on the 25th of February,
Maj. Winston joined Green's army with
a detachment of 100 men, and "these
riflemen of Surry were the very last to
leave the field" on which was given that
"fatal wound to royal authority from
which it lingered and lingering died, on
the 19th day of October, 1781," at Yorktown.

After the Revolutionary War, the
Militia became less necessary for the pro-

tection of the country, but the organization was continued. In 1831 the "Second Regiment of Stokes County Militia" was commanded by Col. Joseph W. Winston, son of Major Joseph Winston.

The following year a committee of five was appointed "to regulate the lines between each Captain's company," and, later, it was "ordered by the Court Marchiel that the Judge advocate shall Furnish Every Captain In the South Ridgement With A Copy of the Destrick or baunds to which he belongs or Commands by next Drill at Salem In May 1834 which was done by the Judge advocate on the 2 day of May 1834." These Captains' Districts, nine in number, could hardly be considered as the predecessors of the townships, although they occupied to some extent the same localities as the townships which were formed after the war. They were simply divisions of the land, apportioning a number of men to each Captain's Company, the lines running as seemed convenient along roads, by streams, around plantations and down lanes. The boundaries were frequently altered and new districts formed, there being 17 in January, 1862, with about 1,635 men enrolled.

The Legislature of 1848–1849 enacted that all men between 35 and 45, while remaining liable to duty in case of war, might secure certificates freeing them from drills, etc., in times of peace. There were usually two General Musters a year, the first being in April or May, the second in October or November. Soldiers were fined for non-attendance by their Company Court Martials, with right of appeal to the Regimental Court Martial. The General Musters were held in Salem in 1831, '32 and '34; in Germanton in 1833 and '35; in Salem in 1836; in Bethabara from 1837–'43 ; in Liberty from 1844–'47 ; in Salem from 1848–'50, and were removed permanently to Winston in 1851. The officers of each company were elected annually, all the companies voting for the field officers.

The Colonels Commandant between
1831 and 1862 were—

Col. Ziglar,
Col. John Flynt,
Col. J. A. Stafford,
Col. M. Masten,
Col. J. W. Alspaugh,
Col. Joseph Masten.

When Stokes County was divided, the
Second or South Regiment of Stokes
County Militia became the *Forsyth
County Militia*, the 66*th Regiment of
North Carolina Militia*, which was later
changed to the 71*st Regiment, North
Carolina Militia*. The Forsyth County
Militia, as such, was not called out dur-
ing the war, and Militia elsewhere in the
State only rarely, and for a short time.
After the war there was an attempt to
reorganize the Militia, but its place was
ultimately taken by the volunteer com-
panies composing the State Guard.

CHAPTER X.

FORSYTH AND THE CIVIL WAR.

On December 20th, 1860, after many years of sectional misunderstanding in the country at large, where political jealousies had fanned a flame that various compromises had temporarily allayed but could not quench, the State of South Carolina seceded from the Union, believing that a "Soverign State" should peacefully withdraw from a union in which it no longer found just treatment or advantage. Mississippi, Florida, Alabama, Georgia, Louisiana and Texas quickly followed, and on February 18th, 1861, Jefferson Davis, of Mississippi, was inaugurated President of the *Confederate States of America.*

No one knew what stand the North would take, so, for the security of the

new government, the Confederate Congress, on the 28th of February, authorized the President

"to receive into the service of this Government such forces now in the service of said
States (Confederate) as may be tendered, or
who may volunteer by consent of their State
in such numbers as he may require, for any
time not less than twelve months unless sooner
discharged."

Again, on March 6th, " in order to provide speedily forces to repel invasion,"
the President was authorized to employ
the Militia, and ask for and accept the
services of any number of volunteers, not
exceeding 100,000.

On March 4th, Abraham Lincoln was
inaugurated President of the United
States, and on April 15th, he issued a
proclamation calling for 75,000 men to
suppress "combinations" in the seven
seceding States, by which the execution
of the laws of the United States were
being obstructed. Six of the border
States refused this demand on their Militia in no measured terms, Governor
Ellis, of North Carolina, writing—

" Your dispatch received, and, if genuine, which its extraordinary character leads me to doubt, I have to say, in reply, that I regard the levy of troops made by the Administration for the purpose of subjugating the States of the South as in violation of the Constitution, and a usurpation of power. I can be no party to this wicked violation of the laws of the country, and to this war upon the liberties of a free people. You can get no troops from North Carolina."

Two days after the appearance of the Proclamation, Virginia withdrew from the Union, North Carolina followed on the 21st of May, and, with Tennessee and Arkansas, joined the Confederate States.

In the organization of the army it was the intention that the troops sent by the various States should come in companies, or, if sufficiently numerous, in regiments, commanded by their own officers, the general officers to be appointed by the government.

At first, this was not always done, and a good deal of complaint was made, but later the companies for each regiment, and even each brigade, were from the same State, and commanded by officers from that State.

During 1861 there were as many volunteers as the Confederate Government could arm, but by the close of that year it became apparent that the struggle would be protracted and severe, and that a more permanent and larger army was a necessity. Congress therefore, in March, 1862, authorized the President to call out all white men between 18 and 35 years of age, for three years of service, those already enlisted for one year to have their time extended ; and on March 13th, Gen. Robert E. Lee was " charged with the conduct of the military operations of the armies of the Confederacy," under the direction of President Davis.

The "Conscription Act" raised a storm in several States, particularly in Georgia and North Carolina, where it was considered an invasion of States Rights, Governor Vance even going so far as to threaten to call out the Militia to resist the conscript officers. This objection

was a legal one, and arose from no luke-
warmness in the cause of the Southern
States, into whose armies North Carolina sent 89,344 volunteers, in addition
to the 30,000 men enlisted under the
severel Conscription Acts, altogether
about one-fifth of her whole white population.

On September 27th, 1862, a call was
made for all men between 35 and 45
years old, and February 11th, 1864, the
age limit was extended to 17 and 50, the
boys from 17 to 18 constituting the Jun-
ior Reserves, and men from 45 to 50 the
Senior Reserves,and all were enlisted "for
the war." While the earlier volunteer
was able to join any company he wished,
if he had a preference, the conscript was
sent to any regiment from his State that
needed refilling, so that men from the
same town might be serving in widely
separated fields.

Meanwhile President Lincoln had
issued his Proclamation of Emancipation
on January 1st, 1863, and on March 3d,

1863, a Northern Conscription Act called
out all Northern men between 18 and
45 to join the army.

Forsyth County sent its full quota of
soldiers to the front, and shared in all
the anxieties and privations of the times,
but was spared the horror of becoming a
battlefield. Parents in less favored districts regarded it as a place of refuge,
and sent their daughters to the Boarding
School in Salem, until that Institution
was full to overflowing and could receive
no more. Gov. Vance showed the School
every courtesy in his power, supplying it
with sugar, etc., from captured stores,
and arranging that Mr. Augustus Fogle,
the School's Steward, should be exempt
from military duty in order to serve the
daughters of the South.

A few other men were detailed to
superintend the work in the Salem
Woolen Mill, which was run to its full-
est capacity to furnish the much needed
" Confederate Gray " for the soldiers in
the field.

On March 20th, 1865, *Stoneman's Raid* started from East Tennessee. Of this and two similar expeditions sent out about the same time, Gen. Grant wrote:

"They were all eminently successful, but without any good result. Indeed much valuable property was destroyed and many lives lost at a time when we would have liked to spare them. Stoneman entered North Carolina and then pushed north to strike at the Virginia and Tennessee Railroad. He got upon that road, destroyed its bridges at different places, and rendered the road useless to the enemy up to within a few miles of Lynchburg. He then pushed south, and was operating in the rear of Johnston's army about the time that negotiations were going on between Sherman and Johnston for the latter's surrender."

As Stoneman marched into North Carolina the news of his coming preceded him, striking terror to the hearts of the people whose defenders were far away. It was expected that he would reach Salem about the first of April, and scouts were posted all along the road to the Shallow Ford, that notice might speedily be given when he crossed, but after an anxious waiting news came that he had turned toward Virginia.

A few days later however, as he marched south, the entire body passed through Forsyth. About 5,000 men, with Gen. Stoneman in command stopped for three hours in Bethania, the General making his headquarters at the home of Mr. Elias Schaub. It being Monday of Easter Week (April 10th,) the Bethania people were all in church when the word came that, all unexpectedly, the Yankees were entering the upper end of the town, and when Rev. Jacob Siewers dismissed the congregation the streets were already filled with soldiers, who burst open doors and rummaged through drawers, but did no serious damage beyond the usual taking of horses. Of these only one escaped, and that because Mr. Schaub appealed directly to Gen. Stoneman for protection, which was granted. After eating everything that could be procured, the party moved on to the Yadkin, crossing at Shallow Ford.

At Winston, the county seat, the Superior Court should have been in session,

but the Minute Docket gives no record
of cases tried, only the following state-
ment, signed by John Blackburn, the
Clerk of the Court.

" The second Monday after the fourth Monday of March, A. D. 1865 Being the 10th day of
April.

Be it remembered that the above mentioned
10th day of April A. D. 1865, is the regular time
of holding the Superior Court of Law of the
County of Forsyth at the Court House in
Winston. And the Clerk and Sheriff T. J.
Wilson & D. H. Starbuck also Jurors witness
suitors &c attended no Judge Soliciter or any
other Attornies attended considerable excite-
ment & many reports concerning the arrival of
the Federal army in town was in circulation
during the day and after waiting patiently for
the Judge to come until the middle of the
afternoon & information being received that
the Yankee army was assuredly on its way not
very far distant, the people began to disperse
rather unceremoniously not taking time to bid
their friends adieu, I consulted some of my
friends about what I should do with records
& papers in the Superior Court Clerk's office
and on consultation concluded to remove the
most valuable, and moved some of my dockets
& placed them in the care of Mrs. Emily Webb,
wife of James Webb, & some with Mrs. Eliza-
beth Long Widow who lived in part of the

7

large Brick building west of the Courthouse
known as Millers Storehouse. One of the
dockets I handed in much haste to my friend
George H. Flynt and requested him to do the
best he could to save it he left it with my friend
F. L. Gorrell Esq. Some of the most valuable
papers I tumbled into a sack and left them
with Mrs. Long at this time great Confusion
prevailed it being certain the army was not far
distant Capt. W. A. Albright Enrolling Officer
had a considerable Confederate Guard in the
Courthouse & they left precipitately I locked
up the office and started down street to hear
the news in Salem. Met Robert De Schweinitz
principal of the Female Academy in Salem
Joshua Boner Mayor of Salem, Thos. J. Wilson
Mayor of Winston and R. L. Patterson, Esq.
who was on a visit to Salem, on their way up
street to meet the Yankee Army. They invited
me to accompany them and we went up street
into Liberty in front of the house then occupied by Mr. Alexander Bevel and halted there
& waited the arrival of the army which was
about or near sundown. The first to come
was ten or fifteen men on horse back Pistols
in hand in full gallop on their arrival in forty
or fifty yards we raised white handkerchiefs
to let them know our mission was peace they
replied all right. they was angry & inquired
for Confederate or rebel soldiers said they had
been fired on other parties came up soon & it
was not long until Gen'l Palmer and Staff
arrived when one of our company introduced

himself to Gen'l Palmer & then introduced the others to him & he introduced us to several of his officers &c & invited us to accompany him into town which we did the main army encamped near the Salem Bridge on the east [south] side of the Creek. Gen'l Head quarters was at the residence of Joshua Boner Esq in Salem."

The Memorabilia of the Moravian Church for 1865 also gives an account of the visit of General Palmer's Brigade.

"After we had enjoyed the solemn meetings on Pa'm Sunday we were greatly startled the next day, April 10th, by the intelligence that the same part of the Federal army looked for on the 3rd would pass through Salem, and indeed toward evening about 4 o'clock they appeared all at once in our midst."

Scouts had been sent out to watch for their approach, and when the Yankees saw them across the hills there was a race for town, in the course of which one man was captured. He was taken to the Federal camp, but was released next morning.

" Before we could realize it soldiers were seen at every corner of the streets, had taken possession of the post-office, and secured our whole town. Some of our brethren had gone

out to meet Gen'l Palmer, the Commander of
the troops coming our way, and our Mayor,
Bro. Josh. Boner, addressed him personally.
When commending our town and community
to his protection, not only on our own account
but also on account of our large female boarding school, the General assured him that no
destruction of any kind would be allowed, and
that we might feel perfectly secure from harm
during their stay with us. Gen'l Palmer established his headquarters in the house of our
Bro. Josh. Boner. In very great, comparative,
silence about 3,000 cavalry passed through our
town, pitching their tents on the high ground
beyond the creek. Had it not been for the
noise their horses and swords made it would
have been hardly noticed that so large a number of—at the time—hostile troops were passing through our streets. The strictest discipline was enforced, guards rode up and down
every street, and very few indeed, comparatively, were the violations of proper and
becoming conduct on the part of the soldiers.''

Guards were also stationed at all the
principal buildings in town, and Mr.
Augustus Fogle, the Steward of Salem
Female Academy, used to enjoy relating
his experiences with the soldier who was
put in charge of the Academy. Finding
him little more than a boy and tired out

from his long march, Mr. Fogle put him
to bed, where he slept serenely until an
officer came by and excitedly demanded
his whereabouts. Being ushered into
the room, the officer was completely
amazed, and exclaiming, " A soldier in
an enemy's country asleep in an enemy's
bed!" jerked the young fellow to the
floor and ordered him off to camp.

Throughout the town "the night was as
quiet as any other, except that there was a
great deal of riding to and fro in Main Street,
and some of us could not divest themselves of
apprehensions that they and their houses
would be in imminent danger in case the cotton factories in town should be molested.
Providentially government stores were in town
in considerable abundance, so that individuals
were not called upon to furnish anything
except bread and the like, for which the men
would generally ask politely and return thanks
in the same manner. No outrages of any kind
(except the pressing of horses) were commit-
ted, and even the cotton manufactories were
spared by the Federals. Without any fault
on the part of their officers, entrance was
effected into one of these establishments, and
a considerable damage was done. During the
afternoon of the 11th a large number of the
Federals came back from the railroad, which

they had tapped in several places. By some
mistake they came into the graveyard avenue
and passed through the graveyard and part of
the cemetery, having shifted their camp to a
place above town, but passing through those
hallowed grounds almost all of them dis-
mounted and led their horses, some even un-
covered their heads. Before dark they had
all left, passing through Winston towards the
river, and though other soldiers, said to be
less disciplined than Palmer's Brigade, have
been near our town, they were not permitted
to enter it. Nevertheless prudence directed a
measure of precaution, especially against
stragglers from Johnston's army, and for some
time our own people kept watch during the
night, and by the Lord's kind assistance all
evil was averted.

The Confederate armies under Lee having
surrendered [April 9th, 1865], portions of them
passed through our town every day. They
were of course under no discipline, and rendered watchful care necessary.

On the 20th of April a number of Confeder-
ates made their appearance, pretending to be
in search of government cloth, to find which
they had intended to search individual houses.
As had been agreed upon the different bells
were at once rung, and in a very short time a
by no means inconsiderable number of men,
many of them soldiers themselves who had
come back on parole, assembled near the
square, armed as well as circumstances per-

mitted, and fully determined to resist the entrance into private houses. Our unbidden
visitors soon changed their language, and
withdrew after a short time without offering
any molestation at all."

General Lee's surrender was soon followed by the capitulation of the other
Southern armies. Gen. Johnston surrendered on April 26th, and on May 4th
Gen. Richard Taylor, who was the senior Confederate officer east of the Mississippi, surrendered everything in his
extensive command, and on May 26th
Gen. E. Kirby Smith did the same for
the trans-Mississippi department, leaving no armies free to continue the war.

Of those who went out from Forsyth
into the struggle the writer of the Memorabilia says:

"As the Lord our God thus exercised His
gracious, guardian care over us who had remained at home, our numerous brethren, sons
and friends who were away from us were also
mercifully protected by Him.

"Our loved ones returned one after the other,
and when we consider how many of them there
were, and to what dangers, hardships and privations they were exposed, and how wonder-

fully they were taken care of, and almost all of them allowed to return to the bosom of their families, surely we must exclaimed with one heart and one voice: "Bless the Lord, O my soul, and forget not all His benefits!"

On the 14th of May the 10*th Regiment of Ohio Volunteers* began a longer stay in Winston and Salem, and Col. Saunders established his headquarters in the house then occupied by Mr. Edward Hege and now by Dr. J. W. Hunter. They left the town on July 13th, and " although upon the whole they had conducted themselves tolerably well as a body, still little regret was felt at their departure, in as much as it had appeared very plainly that their presence was anything but necessary or pleasant, and their moral influence was anything but beneficial."

On the 29th of May Wm. W. Holden was appointed provisional Governor of North Carolina, to hold office until the "loyal people" of that State should be able to restore it " to its constitutional relations to the Federal Government," which restoration was not accomplished until June 25th 1868, when Congress passed an Act receiving the State once more into the Union, the State Legislature having ratified the Fourteenth Amendment to the Constitution of the United States, whereby suffrage was extended to the former slaves.

In 1866 the 100th Anniversary of the founding of Salem was appropriately celebrated in the Moravian Church, by a large concourse of people. Shortly after this festival a strong movement was inaugurated to prohibit the sale of intoxicating liquors in Salem. An appeal was made to the Court of Pleas and Quarter Sessions, who agreed not to issue further license if the vote of the people showed that to be their wish. An election was held on March 17th, when "81 votes were cast in favor of prohibition" within the corporate limits, and "only 15 persons could be prevailed upon to vote the other way." Prohibition was therefore established in Salem, and has been the rule ever since.

During the war there had been out-
breaks of Small-pox in various parts of
the country, but Winston and Salem
escaped until the close of 1866 when there
was· quite an epidemic in Salem. A
piece of flannel cloth had been sent from
Richmond to one of the pupils in the
Academy, a few days later she was taken
sick, and before the disease was recognized it had been communicated to a number of others. In those days the facilities
for a proper quarentine were not available
and naturally many of the girls were ill,
and from the School the disease spread
into the town, but throughout the entire
epidemic not a single death occurred.

CHAPTER XI.

TOWNSHIP LINES.

As has been already stated, the Court
of Pleas and Quarter Sessions was abolished after the close of the Civil War,
and its functions (except the judicial)
were transferred to a *Board of County
Commissioners.* The Minute Docket says
of the first meeting of the new Board.

" The Commissioners Elect for said County
met at the Court House in Winston on Saturday July 25th 1868, when the following persons
presents Certificates from General Edw. Canby
commanding second Military District, that
at an Election held in and for the County of
Forsyth State of North Carolina on the 21st
22nd & 23rd days of April 1868, under the authority of the law of the United States of
March 2nd 1867 'To provide for the more efficient government of the rebel States,' and the
laws supplementary thereto and amendatory
thereof, that they was chosen by a majority of
the qualified voters of said County to their
respective offices as follows :

" William B. Doub, County Commissioner,
qualified as such by Jno. P. Vest, United States
Commissioner, by taking oath prescribed in
section 4 article 6 of the Constitution of the
State of N. C. and in accordance with an Act
of the General Assembly of N. C. ratified July
21st 1868.

Geo. V. Fulp, G. H. Renigar, W. A.
Harper, and Aquilla Pitts were then
qualified as County Commissioners by
Wm. Doub; and Geo. Fulp was made
chairman of the Board.. N. S. Cook,
Register of Deeds, gave his bond for
$10,000.00; Augustus Fogle, Coroner,
gave his for $2,000.00; R. Linville, County
Treasurer, and M. Masten, Sheriff, each
$5,000.00; and John Blackburn, Clerk of
Superior Court $15,000.00.

The State Legislature, at its special
session in 1868, and its winter session
1868-9, provided for the regular bien-
nial election of five men as a Board of
Commissioners in each county, defined
the powers of these Boards, and made it
" the duty of the Commissioners to exer-
cise a general supervision and control of
the penal and charitable institutions,

schools, roads, bridges, levying of taxes, and finances of the county " as should be prescribed by law.

In 1876-7 the Legislature enacted that, beginning with the 1st Monday in June, 1884, the choosing of a Board of Commissioners should be entrusted to the Justices of the Peace of each county, who should meet and elect not more than three or less than five persons to serve in that capacity. To this was added the proviso, in 1887, that no Justice should be eligible for election as County Commissioner.

In 1895 the election was again put into the hands of the people of the county, and the number of Commissioners fixed at three ; with the condition that if at any time after the election of the Commissioners as many as five electors of the county should make affidavit before the Clerk of the Superior Court that " they verily believed that the business of the county, if left entirely in the hands of the three Commissioners elected by the

people, would be improperly managed,"
then upon the petition of 200 electors of
the county the judge of the district, or
the judge presiding therein, was to
appoint two citizens of a different political party from the three already chosen,
who should become full members of the
Board.   At the session of 1897 that sec
tion of the Act which provided for
two such additional Commissioners was
repealed.

The first duty laid upon the County
Commissioners by the Constitution of
North Carolina, and the Acts of 1868,
was the division of their respective counties into districts, "to determine the
boundaries of said Districts, and to report
the same to the General Assembly before
the 1st day of January, 1869.   When
this should be done, and the reports
approved by the General Assembly the
districts were " to have corporate powers
for the necessary purposes of local government, and be known as Townships."

The Commissioners were further em

powered " to erect, divide or alter Townships," either by the consent of a certain number of residents of the townships affected, after due advertisement, or by action of the Legislature. The latter method being the easier, has been the one adopted in Forsyth.

On the 10th of April, 1869, the Legislature enacted—

"That the Districts reported by the Commissioners of the following counties of the State to the present session of the General Assembly are hereby approved, & said Districts, in obedience to Art. VII., sec. 3 & 4 of the Constitution, to-wit, * * Forsyth, * * * shall have corporate powers & shall be known as Townships, by the boundaries and by the names respectively designated in said reports."

Mr. M. H. Morris, the County Surveyor, spent twenty-five days in running the line of the new townships, for which service he received $75.00. He made no map of the county, but in 1882 Mr. James T. Lineback, by independent surveys and by the use of Mr. Morris' notes (which bear date of December 28th,

1868), constructed a large map, a copy of which was placed in the office of the Register of Deeds.

The townships did not coincide with the Captain's Districts of an earlier day, but were rectangular, arranged in three tiers of four each,— *Belews Creek, Salem Chapel, Bethania,* and *Old Richmond* on the north, *Kernersville, Middle Fork, Old Town,* and *Vienna* next, and *Abbotts Creek, Broadbay, South Fork,* and *Lewisville* on the south.

Where Middle Fork, Old Town, South Fork and Broadbay should have cornered Winston Township was inserted, the lines corresponding with those of the Winston and Salem Corporations on the north and west, and extending eastward to Abbotts Creek Township, the western line of that township being identical with the original Wachovia survey.

Between Vienna and Old Town, Lewisville and South Fork, the Muddy Creek was made the boundary, elsewhere natural features were not regarded.   Mr.

Morris' notes show that it was the original intention to let the Kernersville Township line drop back a third of a mile to correspond with that of Belews Creek, but Mr. Lineback found that when the line was actually run it was carried with the Abbotts Creek line and Wachovia survey to Belews Creek Township, the offset being made at that corner.

Belews Creek, Salem Chapel, Kernersville, Abbotts Creek and Lewisville Townships remain unchanged; the others have been more or less altered.

On March 11th, 1889, Forsyth County was enlarged, and a new township, *Clemmonsville*, was formed from the annexed portion. The land was taken from the adjoining county of Davidson, lying south of Forsyth, and the Act of the Assembly provided—

" That from and after the ratification of this Act, all that part of Davidson County lying north, northwest, and west of a line starting at a point known as the " plow-handle corner," * * and running west 23¼° south 3

8

miles to a point on the Yadkin River at or below the mouth of Douthit's branch, shall be annexed to Forsyth county."

The Winston Township lines have been altered several times, chiefly to correspond with changes in the corporation limits of Winston and Salem. Of these Salem was the first to be incorporated, the General Assembly of 1856–7 fixing the limit on the north at the Court House Tract, on the south at the Middle Fork of Muddy Creek, and east and west one-half mile from the centre of Main Street.

Winston was incorporated in 1859, being bounded as follows: "On the south by the town of Salem; on the north by a line one-fourth of a mile distant from and parallel with the northern line of the present town of Winston or Court House Tract; on the west by a line running parallel with the streets of Winston, and 1,278 feet from the centre of the Court House; and on the east by a line running parallel with the western boundary and one-half of a mile distant

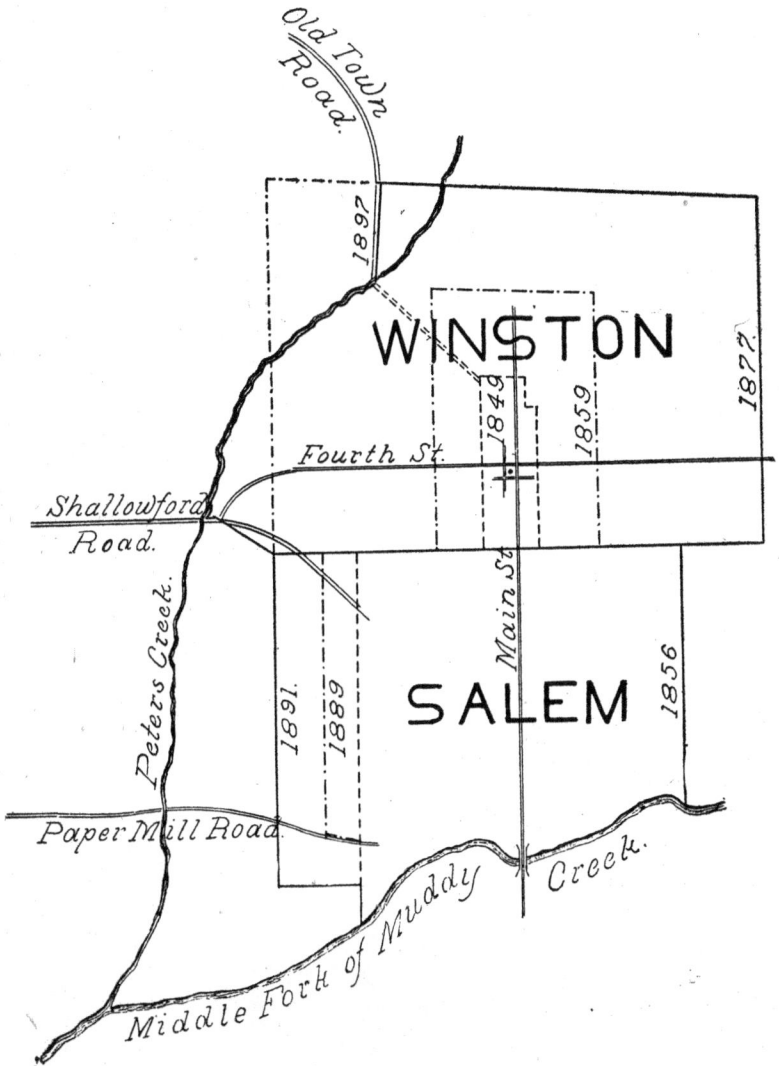

Old Town Road.

1897

WINSTON

1872

1849

1859

Fourth St.

Shallowford Road.

Peters Creek.

1891.

1889.

Main St.

SALEM

1856

Paper Mill Road

Middle Fork of Muddy Creek.

114a

therefrom." These were the lines around Salem and Winston at the time that the townships were surveyed.

At the session of 1876–77 the Winston Charter was revised, and the boundaries widened out, so that they began " at the northeast corner of the corporate boundaries of the town of Salem and southeast corner of the town of Winston, thence running north 80° east 80 poles, thence north parallel with the Winston line 345 poles, thence west one and one-half miles or 480 poles, thence south parallel with the western boundary of Winston 345 poles more or less to a point south 80° west of the northwest corner of the town of Salem, thence north 80° east 80 poles to said north-west corner of Salem, thence north 80° east along the boundary line of Salem and Winston to the beginning." This made Winston fully four times as large as formerly, and considerably increased the territory of the township.

In 1889 Salem extended her limits westwardly, running " with the Winston

Corporation line 500 feet" from the north-west corner of the town of Salem, "thence southwardly and parallel with the present western boundary of Salem to the north side of the old Paper Mill road at the south boundary of Lineback's orchard, thence along the north side of the old Paper Mill road in an eastwardly direction" until it met the old line. Still further advance was made toward the west in 1891, the line beginning at the Winston corner, three-quarters of a mile from the centre of Main Street, and running south 9° east one mile, then north 81° east one-quarter of a mile, thence south 9° east to Middle Fork Creek. Both of these changes involved an alteration in the township line, and the second is the present line of the Salem Corporation and that part of the Winston Township.

The Legislature of 1895 changed the boundary lines of Winston, Middle Fork and Broadbay Townships, enacting that,

"That part of Winston Township lying

south and east of Middle Fork Creek, and
known as the 'pan-handle,' and that part of
Middle Fork Township lying north [south]
and east of Middle Fork Creek, be and the
same is hereby made a part of Broadbay
Township; and that part of Winston Township lying north of Middle Fork Creek and
east of Brushy Fork, be and the same is hereby
made a part of Middle Fork Township."

This made Middle Fork the southern,
and Brushy Fork and the Winston line
the eastern boundary of Winston Township, the northern line remaining as before as far as Brushy Fork.

The present boundary west of Winston was fixed in 1897, when the line running " N. 89° W. along the old corporation line " was stopped at the east side
of the Old Town road, proceeding thence
" in a southerly direction along the east
side of said road to Peters' Creek, thence
in a southwesterly direction down Peters'
Creek to the north side of the Shallowford road to the point at which the road
forks (the north fork running to Winston, and the south fork to Salem), thence
in a southeasterly direction to the north-

west corner of the Salem Corporation."
The portion of Winston Township left
out to the north-west was given to Old
Town Township, and the included part
of South Fork was added to Winston.

In 1895 a new township was created
in Forsyth. Bethania Township received
the name of *Rural Hall*, and a new
township, to be called *Bethania*, was
placed at the point of meeting of Old
Richmond, Vienna, Rural Hall, and
Old Town. It extends "two and a half
miles north, south, east, and west from
the town of Bethania," the east and west
corners of the square falling on the line
between Old Richmond and Vienna,
Rural Hall and Old Town. It was probably the intention that the north corner
should fall on the boundary between
Old Richmond and Rural Hall, but when
surveyed it came a short distance to the
east.

At the present time, therefore, Forsyth County contains fifteen townships.

FORSYTH COURT HOUSE.

CHAPTER XII.

FORSYTH COURT HOUSE.

On the 9th of November, 1895, the County Commissioners—M. D. Bailey, R. S. Linville, and E. W. Hauser—took up a subject which had been attracting the attention of Judges and Grand Juries for five years past, namely, the building of a new Court House for Forsyth County, the old one having become totally inadequate for the purposes for which it was designed.

It was determined to build the new house on the site of the old one, at a cost of $50,000.00, which was later increased to $55,000.00. Frank P. Milburn was accepted as architect, and the contract for construction was given to L. P. Hazen & Co.

It was the original intention to cover

this proposed cost by notes payable in three, four, and five years, secured by a mortgage on the Court House lot, but this was given up, and one. hundred and ten $500.00 Bonds were issued to run five, ten, and fifteen years.

In February, 1896, the old Court House was torn down, the Register of Deeds and Clerk of the Court moving their offices into the Jacobs building, and the Sheriff into the Montague building on Main Street. Court was held in the Armory, and the County Commissioners met in the office of the Register of Deeds while the building was going on, and on the 11th of January, 1897, the new Court House was declared finished and ready for use.

Standing on a slight eminence in the heart of a busy little city, this handsome structure of granite, buff brick and brownstone is as great a contrast to the modest building whose place it took as is the present county seat, with its widespread suburbs, to the three streets and

handful of houses of the " county town "
of 1849, and both speak eloquently of
the great strides that Forsyth County
has made during the fifty years of her
existence.

INDEX.

Abbotts Creek Township............ .... 112, 113
Affirmation of Allegiance.............................. 36, 39
Administrator, Office of........................ 29, 45, 46
Albemarle County..................................... 4, 6
Anson County 6, 10

Bagge, Traugott...................................... 35, 43, 44
Bailey, M. D.. 119
Banner, Constantine L.... .... 64, 66, 74, 76, 80
Bath County... 5, 6
Belews Creek Township.............................. 112, 113
Benzien, Christian Lewis........................ 44, 45, 46
Bethabara 22, 25, 35, 61
Bethania............ .... 26, 96
Bethania Township...................... 112, 118
Blackburn, John 97, 108
Bladen Precinct and County.............................. 6
Blanket Bottom Tract 43
Boner, Joshua...................................... 98, 99, 100
Broadbay Township.............................. 50, 112, 116

CAROLINA—
        Charter of Charles I................................. 3, 82
        Charters of Charles II................. 3, 4, 8
        Grant of George II............................. 9
        North Carolina..................................... 7
        South Carolina..................................... 7
        Purchase of..................................... 8
Carteret, John, Lord..................................... 8
Churton, William.............................. 41, 42

CIVIL WAR—
    Secession... 89
    Confederate States of America................ 89
    Confederate Army............................ 90, 92, 102
    Conscription Act.................................... 92, 93
    Surrender.................................... 102, 103
    Tenth Regiment Ohio Volunteers......... 104

Clarendon County... 4, 5
Clemmonsville Township 113

CONFEDERATE ARMY—
    Volunteers.................................... 90, 92
    Conscripts... 92
    North Carolina Troops............................. 93
    Surrender.................................... 102, 103

Confederate States.................................... 89, 103
Confiscation Act.. 34
Conrad, Leonard... 16
Cornwallis, Lord.................................... 37, 83
Cossart, Christian Frederick........................ 41

COUNTIES—
    Albemarle... 4, 6
    Anson.. 6, 10
    Bath.. 5, 6
    Bladen.. 6
    Clarendon 4, 5
    Craven 4
    Forsyth... 15, 32
    New Hanover.. 6
    Rowan 10, 11
    Stokes 13, 71, 72
    Surry................................... 11, 12, 31, 71

COUNTY COMMISSIONERS—
  Board of.. 107
  First Commissioners........................... 108
  Powers and Duties of.................. 108, 110
  Election of 109
  Court House, Second............................ 119
County Jail... 64, 79
Court House, First................. 54, 64, 76, 120
Court House, Second........................... 119
COURT HOUSE TRACT—
  Commissioners............................. 16, 53, 65
  Site of....................................... 53
  Purchase of............................... 55
  Plan of....................................... 62
  Deed to 55
  Sale of Lots.............................. 63
  Winston...................................... 67
Court of Pleas and Quarter Ses-
  sions..................... 16, 73, 76, 79, 107
Craven County................................... 4
Crooke, Adam.................................. 75
Cunow, John Gebhard.................... 45

Davis, Jefferson........................... 89, 92
Dobbs, Gov. Arthur.................. 19, 23
Dobbs Parish.............................. 25, 31
Dobson's Cross Roads................ 47

Florida.. 3
Fogle, Augustus............. 94, 100, 108
Forsyth, Col. Benj.................... 15
FORSYTH COUNTY................ 15, 16
  Addition to............................ 113

FORSYTH COUNTY—Continued.
　　Civil War............................... 89, 94, 103
　　County Commissioners...................... 107
　　Court House Tract..................... 16, 53
　　Court House, First..................... 54, 76
　　Court House, Second..................... 119
　　Courts..................... 72, 81, 107
　　Early Settlements.... 22, 26, 27, 47, 48, 50, 51
　　Map of..................... 111
　　Militia..................... 82
　　Poor House..................... 66
　　Taxes..................... 74
　　Townships..................... 110
　　Wachovia Tract, Line of............. 25, 31, 112
　　Winston, County Town..................... 67
Friedberg..................... 48
Friedland..................... 50
Fries, Francis..................... 16, 57, 74, 79

Graff, Rev. Michael..................... 43
Grant to Lord Granville..................... 8, 9
Granville, Earl..................... 8, 17, 42
Granville's Line..................... 9, 11
Granville, Sir Robert..................... 30

Hauser, E. W..................... 119
Heath, Sir Robert..................... 3
Holden, William W..................... 104
Hope..................... 51
Horne, Rev. William..................... 43
Hutton, James..................... 18, 29, 34, 39, 41, 45

Inferior Court..................... 81
Indian War..................... 25, 83

Justices of the Peace............................ 72, 81, 109

Kerner, Joseph.. 48
Kernersville 47
Kernersville Township............................ 112, 113
Kluge, Charles F.............................. 46, 55, 66

Lash, Israel..................................... 74
Lash, Jacob..................................... 42
Lease System in Salem.................................. 30, 59
Lemly, Henry A................................. 16
Lewisville Township............................ 112, 113
Liberty.. 87
Lincoln, Abraham.............................. 90, 93
Lineback, James T.................................. 111
Linville, R. S................................. 119
Little Yadkin..................................... 13
Lords Proprietors, Eight..................... 3, 4, 7, 82

Marshall, Frederick William
    von....................... 28, 33, 34, 37, 40, 44, 45, 46
Martin, Gov. Alexander............................. 38
McBride, Jesse......................................75
Meinung, Frederick C.................... 58, 65, 66, 73
Metcalf Lands..................................... 41, 42
Middle Fork Township................... 112, 116
MILITIA—
    Need for........ 82
    Organized..................................... 83
    Revolutionary War.................................. 83
    Colonels Commandant............................. 88
    Second Regiment Stokes County
        Militia................................ 86
    General Musters.................................. 87

MILITIA—Continued.
    Refused to President Lincoln.................... 91
    Civil War.. 88, 90
    State Guard.. 88
Moravian Church.. 17, 31, 36
Moravian Congregation of Salem Incor-
    porated............ 60
Morris, M. H.. 111

New Hanover, Precinct and County............ 5, 6
NORTH CAROLINA.................................... 7, 8, 9
    Militia in Revolutionary War.................. 83
    Secession of.. 91
    Militia in Civil War.................................... 88, 90
    Regulars in Civil War.............................. 90, 91
    Stoneman's Raid.. 95
    Tenth Regiment Ohio Volunteers.......... 104
    Provisional Governor................................ 104
    Re-admitted to Union.............................. 105

Old Richmond Township.......................... 112, 118
Old Town.. 22
Old Town Township.................................... 112, 118

Palmer, General.. 98, 99
Patterson, Rufus L.................................... 98
Poor House.. 66
PRECINCTS—
    Bladen 6
    New Hanover.. 5, 6
Proclamation of Emancipation...................... 93
Prohibition in Salem.................................... 105

Proprietors of Wachovia Tract............ 30, 44, 45
Provincial Elders, Board of........................ 46, 61
Public School Lot.................................... 56, 62

Reichel, Bishop J. F.................................... 37
Revolutionary War...................... 33, 70, 83
Rowan County...................................... 10
Rowan, Matthew.................................. 10
Rural Hall Township.................... 118
SALEM—
    Site of:.................................... 26
    Proposed Plan for............................. 27
    Settlement of....................... 28
    Salem Land.................... 30, 53, 58
    Salem Congregation Diacony...... 58
    Warden, Office of.................. 30
    Visit of Cornwallis................. 37
    Meeting of General Assembly in............. 38
    Visit of George Washington..... 37
    Moravian Congregation Incorporated.... 60
    Provincial Elders, Board of............... 46, 61
    Lease System.................. 30, 59
    Court House Tract................. 16, 53
    Salem Concert Hall................. 72, 80
    Salem Female Academy............ 60, 94, 106
    Stoneman's Raid.................... 95
    Disbanded Soldiers................... 102
    Tenth Regiment Ohio Volunteers......... 104
    One Hundredth Anniversary.............. 105
    Prohibition in................ 105
    Corporation Lines................ 114, 115
Salem Chapel Township.............. 112, 113
9

Salem Congregation Diacony.................................... 58
Salem Female Academy........................ 60, 94, 106
Salem Land.................... 30, 53, 58
Schweinitz, Emil A. de.................................... 46, 60
Schweinitz, Lewis David von.................... 45, 46
Schweinitz, Robert de.................... 98
Secession of North Carolina............................ 91
Shultz, Theodore.................................... 46
South Carolina.................................... 7, 8
Southern Province of the Moravian
   Church.. 31, 61
South Fork Township............................ 112, 118
Spach, Adam.................................... 48
Spangenberg, Bishop Joseph............................ 17
Stafford, John.................................... 16
Stafford, Zadok 16
Starbuck, Darius H............................ 64, 97
Stokes County.................................... 13, 71, 72
Stokes, Judge John.................................... 13
Stoneman's Raid.................................... 95
Surry County............................ 11, 12, 31, 71
Superior Court 75, 81

TOWNSHIPS—
   Division of County............................ 110
   Boundaries and Names,
                     112, 113, 114, 116, 118
Tenth Regiment Ohio Volunteers.................. 104

Unitas Fratrum............................ 17, 19, 36, 44, 62
United Brethren.................................... 39

Van Vleck, William Henry 45

Vienna Township.. 112, 118

Wachovia Sustentation Diacony..................... 60
WACHOVIA TRACT—
    Selection of... 18
    Purchase Money.................................... 18, 20
    Deed to.. 18
    Pioneer Settlers........ 20, 22, 26, 27, 48, 50, 51
    Dobbs Parish...................................... 25, 31
    Indian War... 25
    Salem Land............................... 30, 53, 58
    Administrators........................... 29, 45, 46
    Surry County Line............................... 31
    Revolutionary War................................ 33
    Confiscation Act........................... 34, 39
    Title Transferred................................... 34
    Title Confirmed..................................... 40
    Proprietors........................... 28, 44, 45
    Purchase of Quit-Rents........................ 43
    Wachovia Sustentation Diacony........... 60
    Total Cost of.. 44

Warden, Office of.. 30
Wardens of the Poor.. 65
Washington, George... 37
Wilson, Thomas J........ 54, 56, 64, 65, 73, 97, 98

WINSTON—
    Court House Tract............................... 16, 53
    County Town Named............................ 67
    Court House, First................. 54, 64, 76, 120
    Jail.. 64
    Courts.. 72
    Stoneman's Raid................................... 96

WINSTON—Continued.

Disbanded Soldiers................................... 102
Tenth Regiment Ohio Volunteers. 104
Corporation Lines...................... 114, 116, 117
Court House, Second.................................. 119
Winston, Major Joseph............................... 68, 84
Winston Township 112

Zinzendorf, Count..................... 18, 27, 39